The Water Link

The Water Link
A History of Puget Sound as a Resource

Daniel Jack Chasan

A Washington Sea Grant Publication
Distributed by the University of Washington Press
Seattle and London

First published in 1981 by
Washington Sea Grant Program
University of Washington

Distributed by University of Washington Press
Seattle, Washington 98195

Publication of this book was supported by grants from the National Oceanic
and Atmospheric Administration and by funds from the Environmental
Protection Agency.

The U.S. Government is authorized to produce and distribute reprints for
governmental purposes notwithstanding any copyright notation that may
appear hereon.

Library of Congress Cataloging in Publication Data

Chasan, Daniel Jack.
  The water link.

  (Puget Sound books)
  Bibliography: p.
  Includes index.
  1. Puget Sound region (Wash.)—Industries—
History.   2. Fishery resources—Washington (State)—
Puget Sound—History.   3. Lumber trade—Washington
(State)—Puget Sound region—History.   4. Water—
Pollution—Washington (State)—Puget Sound—History.
I. Title. II. Series.
HC107.W22P838   333.91′64   81-11457
ISBN 0-295-95782-4 (University of Washington Press)
                                        AACR2

ISBN 0-295-95782-4

for Sarah and Matthew

Contents

PUGET SOUND BOOKS

Funds to support the publication of the
Puget Sound Books were provided by the National
Oceanic and Atmospheric Administration (NOAA)
and by the Environmental Protection Agency (EPA).

About the Puget Sound Books

This book is one of a series of books that have been commissioned
to provide readers with useful information about Puget Sound . . .

About its physical properties—the shape and form of the Sound,
the physical and chemical nature of its waters, and the interac-
tion of these waters with the surrounding shorelines

About the biological aspects of the Sound—the plankton that form
the basis of its food chains; the fishes that swim in this inland
sea; the region's marine birds and mammals; and the habitats
that nourish and protect its wildlife

About man's uses of the Sound—his harvests of finfish, shellfish,
and even seaweed; the transport of people and goods on these
crowded waters; and the pursuit of recreation and esthetic fulfill-
ment in this marine setting

About man and his relationships to this region—the characteristics
of the populations which surround Puget Sound; the governance
of man's activities and the management of the region's natural
resources; and finally, the historical uses of this magnificent resource—Puget Sound

To produce these books has required more than four years and the
dedicated efforts of more than one hundred people. This series was ini-
tiated in 1977 through a survey of several hundred potential readers
with diverse and wide-ranging interests.

The collective preferences of these individuals became the standards against which the project staff and the editorial board determined
the scope of each volume and decided upon the style and kind of pre-
sentation appropriate for the series.

In the Spring of 1978, a prospectus outlining these criteria and inviting expressions of interest in writing any one of the volumes was distributed to individuals, institutions, and organizations throughout
Western Washington. The responses were gratifying. For each volume
no fewer than two and as many as eight outlines were submitted for
consideration by the staff and the editorial board. The authors who
were subsequently chosen were selected not only for their expertise in a

particular field but also for their ability to convey information in the manner requested.

Nevertheless, each book has a distinct flavor—the result of each author's style and demands of the subject being written about. Although each volume is part of a series, there has been little desire on the part of the staff to eliminate the individuality of each volume. Indeed, creative yet responsible expression has been encouraged.

This series would not have been undertaken without the substantial support of the Puget Sound Marine EcoSystems Analysis (MESA) Project within the Office of Marine Pollution Assessment of the National Oceanic and Atmospheric Administration. From the start, the representatives of this office have supported the conceptual design of this series, the writing, and the production. Financial support for the project was also received from the Environmental Protection Agency and from the Washington Sea Grant Program. All these agencies have supported the series as part of their continuing efforts to provide information that is useful in assessing existing and potential environmental problems, stresses, and uses of Puget Sound.

Any major undertaking such as this series requires the efforts of a great many people. Only the names of those most closely associated with the Puget Sound Books—the writers, the editors, the illustrators and cartographers, the editorial board, the project's administrators and its sponsors—have been listed here. All these people—and many more—have contributed to this series which is dedicated to the people who live, work, and play on and beside Puget Sound.

Alyn Duxbury and Patricia Peyton
May 1981

Preface

I started this book with the idea of explaining how we got here from there, how the early uses of and attitudes toward Puget Sound evolved into the uses and attitudes of today. When I decided to cover events that had occurred as recently as 1977, I realized that I would have no way of judging their ultimate importance and that most of the people who had participated in them would be alive, well, and fully capable of challenging my interpretations. It is inconvenient to write "history" about recent events. I believe, though, that it's well worth the inconvenience. The history of Puget Sound didn't end with the gold rush, the demise of the sailing ship, or the invention of the chainsaw, and of all the reasons for studying history, learning how the present evolved from the past isn't the least valuable.

Daniel Jack Chasan
September 1980

Left: In the 1870s, men were still felling trees with single-bitted axes. (HSSKC)

Below: Lumberships tied up at Port Blakely about 1900. (HPCUW, Wilhelm Hester photo)

trees to cut and water to float them on

The men who sailed into Puget Sound on the *Julius Pringle* in the summer of 1853 knew exactly what they were looking for and must have had a good idea of what they'd find. They wanted a site on which to build a steam-powered sawmill that could rip lumber for the gold rush boomtown of San Francisco. W. C. Talbot, who was on board the *Pringle*, and his partner, Andrew Jackson Pope, were the sons of logging families in East Machias, Maine, who had sailed for San Francisco at the end of 1849, the year the gold rush started, and had gone into the lumber business there. Buildings were going up all over San Francisco, and there was a great demand for lumber. The boards that had been milled on the East Coast and taken on ships around Cape Horn were very expensive—too expensive to be sold at much of a profit. Pope and Talbot wanted to be able to sell cheaper lumber. To do that, they'd have to mill their own.

In the middle of the nineteenth century, one did not transport wood very far overland. There were no railroads on the Pacific Coast, relatively few miles of track even in the East. To carry logs or large amounts of lumber, one used the water. Pope and Talbot would have to find a source of timber along the coast. They would need not only the timber, which was plentiful enough, but also a deep, sheltered anchorage in which to tie up and load ships. From San Francisco, the closest sheltered spot was Humboldt Bay, in the redwood country of northern California. There was a bar across the entrance of Humboldt Bay, though, and the two partners didn't relish the idea of taking ships across it. The Columbia River, farther north, was blockaded by an even more treacherous bar. Pope and Talbot decided to go all the way north to Puget Sound.

For several years, ships from San Francisco had been visiting the Sound to pick up cargoes of pilings and spars. Some of the timber was cut by the ships' crews and some by little groups of settlers.

The crews had seen the snow-capped mountains looming over the Sound, had seen the killer whales and hordes of salmon, had seen timber that even by the standards of the mid-nineteenth century was all but unbelievable. Douglas firs twelve feet across at the base, a hundred-fifty feet tall, and straight enough for masts were common. Inland, such big

1

trees could not have been moved to market. Here they grew right down to the water's edge.

A sailing ship could put in almost anywhere to pick them up. The water of the Sound rose and fell with the Pacific tides, but it was all sheltered from Pacific storms and currents by the Olympic Peninsula and the southern tip of Vancouver Island. Lying in a glacial trough, the water, in places, was nine hundred feet deep, and no obstructions lay between it and the open Pacific.

The country was so empty that one could set up a mill almost anywhere. The boundary of the Oregon Country, from which the Washington Territory had split off that March, had been settled with Great Britain only seven years before, in 1846. San Francisco itself had been part of the United States only since the end of the Mexican War, in 1848. Farther north, Alaska was still Russian and would remain Russian for fourteen more years. The northwestern corner of the country was extremely remote. There were no transcontinental railroads, no telegraph lines. Even the pony express was seven years in the future. The opening of the Panama Canal was more than sixty years in the future. To get from the East Coast to the West Coast, one took a sailing vessel around Cape Horn, traveled overland by wagon or on foot, or else took a ship to Panama, made one's way through the jungles of the isthmus, then took another ship north to San Francisco; to reach the Columbia River or Puget Sound, one changed ships again.

In 1846, when the Oregon Country was established, there were said to be only eight white men living in U.S. territory beyond the north bank of the Columbia River. The only settlement was a Hudson's Bay Company trading post near the mouth of the Nisqually River. (There were also Hudson's Bay Company trading posts on Vancouver Island and beside the Fraser River, as well as Fort Vancouver on the north bank of the Columbia.) The shores of Puget Sound belonged to Indians, whose economy was oriented toward the water. Salmon was the great staple. Every river flowing west from the Cascade Mountains or east from the Olympics into Puget Sound had its own run of salmon or steelhead trout, and the giant salmon runs of the Fraser River, just above the Canadian border, passed through the Strait of Juan de Fuca and the upper Sound. Bands of Indians lived at the mouths of the rivers. In addition to the salmon, they took halibut, cod, and other fish from the salt water, and gathered shellfish along the rock beaches at low tide.

The federal government didn't formally acquire the land around Puget Sound from the Indians until 1854 and 1855, but by 1853, when Washington became a separate territory, it was obvious that white civilization was there to stay. Millard Fillmore was in the White House then, and Franklin Pierce was about to enter it. The extension of slavery into new territories was the nation's main political issue. In Europe,

Britain, Turkey, and France were fighting against Russia in the Crimean War. It was only a year after Commodore Perry sailed across the Pacific to open trade with Japan, eight years before the Civil War. There were still living men and women who could remember the American Revolution. The United States was young, although English-speaking people had been living on the East Coast for a very long time. Harvard University was already 217 years old.

On the shores of Puget Sound, white civilization still barely existed. A few small groups of people lived in log cabins at the edge of the towering woods, just beyond the beaches. They used single-bitted axes to chop down trees so large that the ground shook when they fell. There was a water-powered sawmill at Tumwater, small ones at the current sites of Bellingham and Tacoma; however, until 1852 and 1853, the closest thing most settlers had to an industry was squaring off fallen logs with hand saws—two men to a saw, one standing in a saw pit below the log and one standing above.

Conserving the trees was not a thought that could have entered anyone's mind. Figuring out how to use them was the problem. The trees were essential for building cabins and making fires, but they had no cash value in a strictly local economy. Nor was there anyone within five hundred miles who needed or would pay for them. The settlers' only hope of translating those trees into money was their access to water, to ships bound for places where people had more dollars and less wood. The trees and the water were to dominate the region's attention and energy for generations. They were never to absorb the full range of human activity or consciousness around the Sound, but they were to be central. The Sound itself was and would remain central in the most literal sense: the towns were on the outside and the water was in the middle. There was no upstream or downstream, no linear procession of communities strung out along a north-south coast. In the 1850s and for more than a century afterward, the people who lived beside the Sound viewed the water as a conduit that could—and ideally would—bring economic development to their doorsteps, no matter how remote their doorsteps might be.

Talbot and the crew of the *Julius Pringle* would have preferred a mill site that was as close as possible to the Pacific and therefore to San Francisco, but that wasn't their main consideration. At a time before the Panama or even the Suez Canal had been built, people were used to long, looping voyages. At a time when most ships were still powered by wind, a few extra miles didn't require extra fuel. The most important considerations were good stands of timber and a safe anchorage.

The *Julius Pringle* anchored in Discovery Bay, near the future site of Port Angeles. From there, Talbot and his men took a small sailboat and an Indian canoe farther into the Sound to scout additional shores

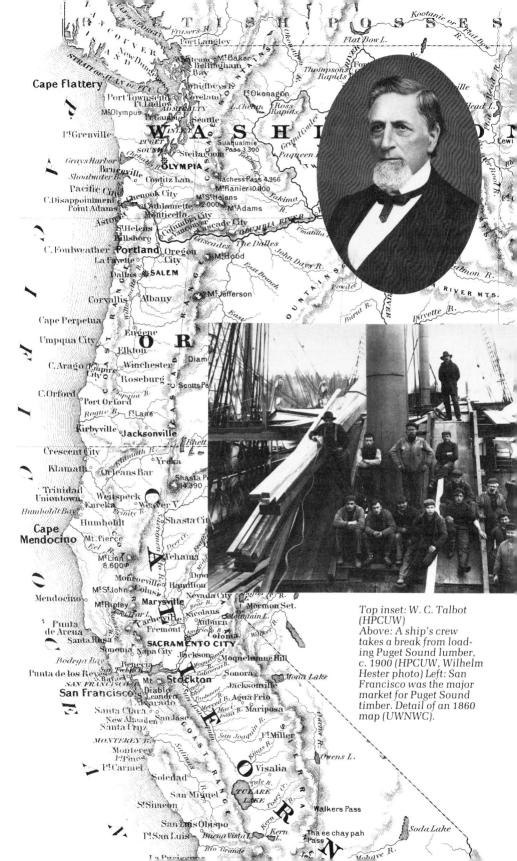

Top inset: W. C. Talbot (HPCUW)

Above: A ship's crew takes a break from loading Puget Sound lumber, c. 1900 (HPCUW, Wilhelm Hester photo) Left: San Francisco was the major market for Puget Sound timber. Detail of an 1860 map (UWNWC).

and islands, including those now called Bainbridge and Vashon. They eventually chose the spot that was to become Port Gamble, on the northeastern shore of Hood Canal. It had everything they were looking for: a deep anchorage, thrice-sheltered from the open Pacific within the Strait, the Canal and a curve of shoreline; a long, straight view toward open water; and miles of virgin timber behind the beach. Talbot left a crew to assemble the mill and sailed back to San Francisco.

By the end of 1853, steam sawmills were ripping timber into boards at Port Gamble, Port Ludlow, Appletree Cove, Alki, and Seattle. These and later steam sawmills were the economic life of the Sound. People caught fish, farmed in the clearings, made an effort to salt and ship salmon, made some lime, raised some sheep, sold things to each other—but the mills were the focus of it all. Referring to that early period, Norman Clark has written of "the sawmills that became Seattle, Olympia and Port Townsend."

Even those early mills could turn out thousands of board feet of lumber a day. The closest significant market for the lumber—and the spars and pilings that were still being cut—was San Francisco, hundreds of miles away. Other lumber went to Hawaii and the Orient. In 1855, a mill which cut spars for the French and Spanish navies, was established at Utsalady, on the northern tip of Camano Island.

Clippers and other big sailing ships carried cargo and passengers to destinations outside the Sound. Within the Sound, settlements were tied together by a continual traffic of smaller craft. Animals, hay, lumber and shingles (for local use), lime, clothing, and all the other necessities of life were hauled back and forth across the water.

It is hard to imagine the immense scale of the looming forests and the tiny scale of human activity around the Sound. Even for the most successful pioneers, life must have been full of petty frustration. In May of 1858, for example, the leading pioneer of Bellingham, Henry Roeder, wanted to go to Port Townsend, the site by then of the federal customs house, to catch the clipper *Live Yankee* for a trip to San Francisco. At the time, he was using a scow, the *H. C. Page*, to haul cargo around the Sound. On Thursday, he "left home in the scow for Semiahmee about two o'clock; arrived the same night [at] 12 P.M." The next day, he "unloaded the scow to start for Port Townsend, but Crist [sic] left her aground, so we were detained until the tide rose again." He very nearly missed his connections as a result. On Saturday morning, he "left Semiahmee at 4 A.M. and had a good leading wind from the West. Arrived at Port Townsend at 2 P.M. and the *Live Yankee* was just starting for San Francisco, so Mr. Page and myself went on board from the scow."

Boat service on the Sound was vital, but scheduling was necessarily casual. Even when Roeder wasn't trying to make connections with a clipper, sailing his scow around the Sound was fraught with problems of tide and weather and human foibles. A few years later, heading down the Sound, he camped for the night, then "got underway at 6 A.M. at Vashon Island; arrived at Steilacoom [then a major settlement] at 10 A.M. Took on 15 hides at Rudolphs and started for Olympia; came to anchor near falls." Two days later, still in the vicinity of the falls, he "arrived at the mill at 4 P.M. Took in two tons flour and 500 pound shorts." He thought he was set to go, but the next day, he noted, "Patterson drunk and would not bring the cattle." On Friday, "Paterson drunk; came down from the mill to Kindall's Company wharf." On Saturday, "The cook and Bill are drunk; Rain all day." Finally, on Sunday, "Took the 29 head of cattle and one pony for Colonel Patterson at Olympia wharf. Left at 10:30 P.M. Arrived at Steilacoom 2 P.M.; left 4 P.M. Arrived at Seattle at 12 P.M."

One didn't always have to contend with drunkenness among shippers or crew—although Roeder certainly didn't seem shocked to encounter it—but given the scale of activity around the Sound, one did always have to contend with individuals.

One also had to contend, time and time again, with the weight, the bulk, the sheer immobility of the first-growth logs. A big fir or cedar log couldn't be moved far through the forest. Teams of oxen could drag the massive thing along a skid road, a local invention consisting of greased, smaller logs set in the ground at right angles to the path of the log being moved. But one could skid a log only so far. The ideal was to drop the trees into, or almost into, the Sound. There, they could be towed easily to the mill or loading point.

When coal was discovered near the Sound during the 1860s, the same principle applied. Coal was, if anything, even harder to move around than logs. A mine had to be close either to the Sound or to inland bodies of water that were near the Sound. The early mines at Bellingham were near the dock. Similarly, early mines east of Seattle were near Lake Washington, from which the coal could be hauled laboriously to Lake Union, from which it could be hauled laboriously to the Seattle piers.

Writing from the perspective of 1914, a commissioner of the Port of Seattle designated the years from 1851 to 1853 as the period of squared timbers, from 1853 to 1864 as the period of sawn lumber, and from 1864 to 1883 as the period of coal shipments. The coal industry really did become important at that time, but to speak of a coal "industry" and to speak of the tonnage shipped from Bellingham or Seattle is probably to mislead the modern reader. An industry it may have been, but big business in any modern sense it was not. Roeder hauled coal on his scow. His diary entry for October 3, 1861, begins by noting an order for five tons of timothy hay to be carried from Whidbey Island to Whatcom (one of the communities that later became Bellingham) and ends by noting, "Loading coal at mines; one Indian at work." The following January, he writes, "Went into the mine and commenced loading coal for up Sound. George Warner and Dan House helped loading."

Important though the coal trade may have been to a few communities, the shipment of lumber and logs remained the main economic activity of the Sound. The mill companies bought logs from independent loggers, to whom they also advanced credit and sold provisions. Ships from all over the world would tie up at the mill piers. At the edge of the Sound, surrounded by stumps and mud, big circular saws would whine from dawn to dusk.

By the standards of the time and place, the major mills were very big business indeed. They did not command much capital, though, and they often worked very close to financial disaster, economizing as best they could and operating on the smallest feasible investments. In 1876, the management of the Port Blakely Mill on Bainbridge Island wrote to Dan Turner in Olympia, asking him to "get us out all you possibly can of good nice, clear sticks from 50 to 70 feet long. . . . When you have out 30 sticks let us know and we will send for them. We will want 100 of the sticks. Get them out as soon as possible. After you have obtained the sticks reduce your force to the lowest possible working gang and cut expenses as low as possible." This from the operators of the largest single sawmill in the world.

The companies built their little empires on resources that were free or almost free. Timber was stolen outright from public lands or cut from land that had been withdrawn from the public domain by individual claims, then sold immediately to the timber companies. A particularly handy means of acquiring timberland was provided by the federal Timber and Stone Act, passed in 1878. The Act enabled any citizen, for the price of $2.50 an acre, to acquire 160 acres of public land suitable chiefly for the harvesting of timber. It didn't take the companies long to turn the legislation to their own advantage. Legions of individuals all over the West acquired cheap public timber on their behalf. No matter how the timber was obtained, once it was cut, it was transported on the free public waters of the Sound.

Beside those public waters, the mill owners erected a string of company towns. "Along the entire length of the Sound are scattered towns containing from 100 to 300 inhabitants, in which no business but that of lumber is carried on," noted an 1872 *Business Directory and Guide to Washington Territory*. "These mills are owned principally by firms in San Francisco, many of whom are quite wealthy in lands. . . . A few of the mill companies purchase the hewn timber from those who make a business of logging, and manufacture lumber, while others hire their own loggers. . . . The proprietors of the mills own the site of the town in which their establishments are situated, and no business but

Port Ludlow was one of the many milling towns that grew up around Puget Sound (HPCUW, Gifford).

such as they choose is permitted on their property. They generally own the store, hotel or boarding house, so monopolize whatever money may be spent by the employees. . . . The towns are generally situated in some sheltered nook, with deep water in front, and often are imperceptible until you come directly abreast them. All are furnished with a school-house, and a church or public hall in which religious services are held. [Utsalady, where spars were still being exported and a steam sawmill had been operating since 1855, also boasted a skating rink.] Shipbuilding is carried on at every town, and often two or three crafts of various kinds are on the stocks at once. . . . The number of ships awaiting cargoes in the towns is a matter of surprise to strangers, the contrast being so great between the small forest of masts and the few scattering houses discernible. Were it not for the heavy puffing of the steam the towns would seem to be Arcadian hamlets."

The *Directory*—a remarkably interesting document published in Olympia by Murphy and Harned—listed only five Sound communities that weren't company owned: Seattle, Port Townsend, and three places at the southern end of the Sound, Olympia, Tumwater, and Steilacoom. Everyplace else, including Tacoma, was a "milling town." The list of "milling towns" included Port Gamble, Port Ludlow, Uniontown, and Seabeck on Hood's Canal; Port Discovery on the tip of the Olympic Peninsula; Utsalady on Camano Island; Coupeville and Coveland on Whidbey Island; and Whatcom, La Conner, Snohomish City, Cadyville, and Mukilteo on the upper Sound.

No community around the Sound had even two thousand inhabitants at the time. Except for the mills and the coal mines, there was little industry, and only the mills represented any appreciable concentration of capital. Two decades after the first steam sawmills started up, trees were still felled with single-bitted axes, and logs were still being skidded to the water by teams of oxen. There were plenty of fish to catch, but mostly they were sold fresh to local residents. The salmon that found their way to California or more distant markets were salted and packed in barrels. The big new industrial venture at the time the 1872 *Business Directory* was published was a plant for the extraction of oil from dogfish. Europe would pay seventy-five cents a gallon for the oil, and the Sound was full of dogfish, so a San Francisco company had set up weirs and processing machinery on McNeil Island, near Steilacoom.

Although ships were the lifeblood of the Sound and every community had some facilities for building them, no place had a drydock capable of handling large ships or complex mechanical repairs. If a steamer had any serious mechanical problems, she had to be taken south to San Francisco.

From the earliest settlement through the 1870s, the whole economy of the Sound was oriented toward San Francisco. Businessmen and workers might, like Pope and Talbot, have come from Maine, from other places in the Northeast, or from Canada, Britain, or northern Europe; however, most of the capital came from the city in California. Pope and Talbot maintained their headquarters there. So did Renton, Holmes and Company, the owners of the Port Blakely Mill. San Francisco was the main market for Puget Sound coal and salted salmon, as well as its lumber, and the point from which milling and other machinery was sent. It must have seemed natural that San Francisco was also the place for major ship repairs.

Despite the vigor of the people who settled near the Sound and their capacity to work long days with axes, hammers, shovels, and saws, they were in some ways extremely passive: they were always waiting for someone else—usually someone in San Francisco—to send in capital, technology, machines. The region itself provided little more than raw resources and a labor force. Some of that labor force must have been highly ingenious; in the muddy clearings behind the beaches, skilled workmen—some brought from Maine and other old logging centers—filed the big saws, set up machines, and made daily repairs on both milling machinery and steamboats, which represented the most advanced technology of the time. Major ship repairs required more than ingenuity, though, just as outgrowing a primitive frontier economy would require more than physical vigor and a willingness to work.

The lumber industry did, at least, use steam technology to turn the native trees into boards. Salmon—plentiful then beyond the twentieth century's wildest dreams—were still handled in a basically pre-industrial manner. The Indians smoked salmon. The white men salted them. Canning had begun on the Sacramento River in 1866 and on the Columbia in 1872, but on the Sound, the first cannery wasn't built until 1877. It was established at Mukilteo, where more primitive fish packing had been done for years. The promoters of industrial progress welcomed it for several reasons. Not only would it be an asset to the economy; it would also represent an advance from subsistence to capital accumulation, from fishing as a lifestyle to fishing as an expression of energetic Anglo-Saxon business practice.

"Our fisheries have long been considered as chief among our numerous resources," observed the *Seattle Daily Intelligencer* in September 1878, "but probably no interest has been slower of development. Until very recently besides what little has been done by the aboriginal fisheries, this industry has been exclusively in the hands of a considerable number of Slavonic and Greek fishermen. . . . like their ancestors they cast their nets in the morning and dream away the remainder of the day in setting about their numerous fish stands disposing of their limited catch. . . . they are much inferior to the sturdy Anglo-Saxon fishermen of the Atlantic coast. . . . Happily, at last the attention of a more enterprising and thorough-going class of men seems to have been directed toward [the fisheries]. Last year. . . for the first time the experiment of putting up Puget Sound salmon for the San Francisco and other markets was tried. It proved to be an unequivocal success." Finally, there would be something to do with all those salmon. Finally, there would be an incentive to invest significant sums of money in the fishery—and to catch more fish than was biologically wise.

From a distance of more than a century, it is impossible to know just what the *Daily Intelligencer's* editor envisioned. Surrounded by huge trees and a sawmill economy, he referred to the fishery as "chief among our numerous resources." The sheer abundance of the salmon and other sea life must have been overwhelming. Presumably, he reasoned that if one could tap that abundance, one could build a prosperous modern economy based on the Sound. A canning industry may have looked like the first big step in that direction.

Whatever dreams that first salmon cannery inspired, the main development that people had looked forward to since the 1870s began was, of course, the completion of a railroad from the Midwest. In 1864, President Abraham Lincoln had signed a bill offering huge land grants as the reward for constructing a Northern Pacific Railroad from Lake Superior to Puget Sound. Every ambitious city on the Sound wanted to be the terminus of the railroad, which would tie the area to the Midwest and the East for the first time. But the project started slowly, and then the panic of 1873 ruined the railroad's main backer, the financier Jay Cooke. Construction of the Northern Pacific halted for the duration of the 1870s. The Sound remained dependent on sailing ships and steamboats, Pacific markets, and San Francisco capital.

Within the framework of that water-oriented, lightly capitalized, basically colonial economic system, it was clear by the early 1870s that some communities were likely to prosper and others weren't. Olympia, as large as any city on the Sound, closest point to the overland route from the Columbia River, headquarters of the main steamers plying the Sound, had a problem. "The shores of the inlet are steep and bold until they reach within a quarter of a mile of the city, when they shoal suddenly," the 1872 *Business Directory* noted. "A large mud flat extends for a distance of a mile and a half at low tide, and this is the greatest drawback to the place. At high tide, the water is deep enough for any class of vessels, but at low water small boats even are left beached. The consequence of this is that steamers have to come in at high tide and leave on the next." The *Directory* observed that "this defect to navigation can be readily overcome by means of a breakwater or a dock," but it was not. A directory published eighteen years later noted that a "small expenditure of money in dredging out a deeper channel leading to the wharves already built will add immeasurably to the importance of Olympia's traffic with other Sound ports. . . . one cannot help wondering why the Olympians did not bestir themselves at an earlier date."

Seattle had no such impediments. As early as 1872, its role as a center of trade within the Sound—not a center of exports, like Port Gamble and the other major mill towns—seemed to guarantee its future success. "It resembles a suburban New England town," observed the 1872 *Directory*, "were it not for the occasional burnt stumps which lie in spots and the ungraded character of some streets.

"No city on the coast, not possessed of manufacturing interests, . . . does as large a business, proportionate to population. Its merchants . . . extend their commercial relations to all portions of the surrounding country. The commerce of the place will exceed $1 million a year . . . . Occupying . . . a central position on the Sound, it promises to become in the future the commercial metropolis of that section of the country.

"Besides the business done with the surrounding country, Seattle ships large quantities of hay and cereals to Portland. . . . three-fourths of the lumber business of the Sound concentrates within a radius of 35 miles . . . and as the logging camps require a large amount of supplies, Seattle is their depot for procuring them, hence all the agricultural products not needed by the population are consumed by the camps. . . .

"[Seattle's] central location gives it control of all routes of travel by water, so the asthmatic puffs and heavy curling smoke of river boats can be heard and seen on [Elliott] Bay at any hour of the day."

Padraic Burke has observed in *A History of the Port of Seattle* that "in the early . . . days of maritime commerce . . . most trading vessels kept a flexible schedule. . . . When there was produce to move from the farms on Whidbey Island to logging villages up the Sound or a shipment of logs on the Olympic Peninsula had been stacked, the ships moved. . . . Being centrally located . . . Seattle could quickly dispatch ships to either the northern or southern end of the waterway. . . . It was this central location that early attracted a number of small, independently owned schooners and steamships to Seattle. Individually, these ships would not have made a significant contribution . . . but collectively they were of decisive importance.

"Beginning in 1865, Seattle began to establish regular connections with Bainbridge Island ports. This . . . gave Seattle its first individual recognition as a major port on the Sound, and it also began what was to grow into a network of Sound connections. In the fall of that year, James W. Kern, with his sloop, the 'Alexander,' began making regular runs between Seattle and Port Blakely. By 1869, the schooner 'Phantom' made a daily trip between Seattle [and the Bainbridge and Kitsap

Peninsula towns of] Freeport, Blakely, Port Orchard and Port Madison."

The ships may have been busy on the Sound, and lumber may have kept rolling out of the mills, but as the 1870s progressed, the region wasn't outgrowing its frontier economy. There were trees to cut and water to float them on and little else, except for the coal and the bare beginnings of a canning industry. What other economic prospects there had been were shattered by the panic of 1873. Railroad construction ground to a halt, and money grew scarce. In 1878, Schwabacher Brothers and Company of Seattle offered a ten percent discount for cash purchases of clothing and dry goods, advertising the offer as "anticipating the wants of the Public during these Hard Times."

1873 ledger of Washington Mill Company (UW Manuscripts)

Top: In the 1880s, the two-man crosscut saw became the logger's principal tool (HSSKC) Bottom: A railroad construction crew in the Cascades (HPCUW)

a new economic geography

For Puget Sound, the 1880s marked the end of frontier isolation and of strictly frontier levels of investment and production. Life was still lived among mud and stumps against a backdrop of giant trees. The Sound was still ringed with mill-company towns. The rowboat still was and would for decades remain a standard means of transportation; one might row to the store, row to school, row to catch the steamboat, even row across the lower Sound. Nevertheless, the days when economic activity consisted chiefly of felling trees as close as possible to the water were drawing to a close.

The biggest single economic event of the new decade was the coming of the Northern Pacific Railroad to Tacoma in 1883. Tacoma had been a "milling" town to begin with, and now it became largely a railroad-company town. The possession of rail connections eastward gave Tacoma a commercial advantage over every other commmunity on the Sound.

As the completion of the railroad indicated, there was money around again. There was also a wave of technological progress in things large and small. Until the 1880s, trees were felled with axes, then cut into lengths with crosscut saws. In the early 1880s, loggers in the California redwoods discovered that they could use saws to fell the trees, too—and that it was a lot more efficient than using an ax. The method quickly spread north along the coast. The big undercut was still cleared with an ax, but the two-man crosscut saw became the logger's principal tool.

In the mills, mechanical saws became a lot more efficient. Circular saws had been used in the first steam sawmills, and they were used with some modifications for the next thirty years. A different kind of saw, the band saw, had made its first public appearance at the Centennial Exposition in Philadelphia in 1876. By the 1880s, it made its way to the Sound, and the amount of lumber a mill could cut in a day increased ten times.

In fishing, too, productivity increased enormously. The early 1880s saw the establishment of the first fish trap, a funnel of nets supported by wooden pilings into which salmon returning to spawning streams could swim. (The Indians had trapped salmon for centuries;

this was the first white version of a trap.) By far the largest salmon run that passed through any portion of the Sound was the one bound for the Fraser River. To reach the mouth of the Fraser, the salmon swam among the American owned San Juan Islands and past Point Roberts, the American owned promontory just south of the river.

Point Roberts had been known as a good fishing place for generations. Indians had camped there every year, erected drying racks, and caught the returning salmon in reef nets. The fishermen went out in pairs of canoes, each holding one end of a net. When the fish were between the two canoes, the net would be lifted and the fish caught.

The white entrepreneurs erected their traps in the traditional Indian fishing spots. More traps followed. And the trap owners discovered the obvious: traps were a very efficient way of catching salmon. Anyone with a leaky rowboat could still go out and catch salmon, but the person or corporation with enough money to erect a trap could go out and catch many more. It was not likely to be the old Mediterranean fisherman who erected the trap, either. It was likely to be an Anglo-Saxon entrepreneur who also owned a cannery.

A greater capital investment was becoming important in the lumber industry, too. It didn't happen all at once. As the 1880s began, the Port Blakely Mill, for example, was still the core of a company town with some four hundred inhabitants on the southern tip of Bainbridge Island. Logs were towed to it from logging camps all around the Sound, milled into lumber, and loaded on ships bound for ports all over the Pacific. Because the parent company's home office was San Francisco, a constant stream of communication flowed back and forth between California and the mill. The company owned tugs that brought log booms from the distant logging camps, but it did not own the camps themselves.

The new decade notwithstanding, the mill itself was still basically a frontier enterprise that cut corners wherever possible and was largely at the mercy of the elements. At the beginning of 1882, William Renton, who ran the mill, wrote that, "the winter has been the worst we have had for many years as far as logging is concerned. We have had alternate rain and snow for about a month, and in some places the snow is reported quite deep. It is next to impossible to tow logs, either. The Politkofsky [an old Russian gunboat brought from Alaska and used as a tug for many years] was over a week after a raft of cedar and then did not get it—had to let it go [at] Vashon. She has now been away three days after another cedar raft and we don't know whether she has lost it or not. . . . Logs are getting fearfully scarce. . . . it looks now as though we could be compelled to saw anything we can get hold of this spring."

A year later, the problem wasn't too much precipitation but too little. In the summer of 1883, Renton was writing, "The weather is very dry and the whole country seems to be on fire. Several camps have been burnt out, and unless rain comes very soon, we fear that there will be very few saved from the flame. We have a good amount of logs on hand here and at the several camps, but if the fire becomes general we may run short, and for that reason you had better be careful about taking foreign orders. We do not wish to frighten you . . . but if the fire continues we shall be short in the fall. After the fire has passed over the ground it is some time before the logger dares to drive his oxen over it for fear of burning their feet, as the fire remains in the roots."

Inside the mill, one found classical mid-nineteenth-century steam technology—with a few exceptions. Edison had developed the electric light bulb, and in 1882, he set up the very first commercial generating plant on Pearl Street in New York. Private homes in Port Blakely and the other mill towns of Puget Sound wouldn't get electric lighting for years, but in 1882, the Port Blakely Mill ordered a sixteen-light electric generating machine to use inside the mill on dark winter days.

Outside the mill, the equipment was as unprepossessing as ever. The ships used to haul lumber from Puget Sound were never the newest and fastest of their kinds, but some were better than others. Evidently, some of those in the employ of the Port Blakely Mill Company were worse than most. In 1882, Renton wrote the home office that "The Rideout arrived yesterday morning. She is getting very bad. . . . In scraping her top sides some of the planking dropped in and the [captain] has got afraid of her. We think when he gets scared of her it is high time to sell her."

The Rideout wasn't the only thing that seemed to be reaching the end of the line. The Timber and Stone Act, which had provided such a convenient method of putting public timber into corporate hands, was under fire. Abuse of the Act was so widespread and flagrant that a congressional commission had asked for its repeal and there seemed a reasonable chance the Congress would oblige. In 1883, with the Act's political future highly uncertain, the federal government sent an inspector to the Puget Sound region to check on local abuses of it.

Renton saw the handwriting on the wall, but he wanted to delay the inevitable as long as possible. In June 1883, he wrote to the manager at Port Gamble, Cyrus Walker, that the "Governmental Special Agent for homestead, preemption and timber claims is making an examination of all such entries. The [Interior] Department has suspended the issuing of patents on all timber applications until after the agent reports. He is a confidential friend of H. C. Struve. Tacoma will give Struve $100 to have him use his influence to present the matter in as favorable a light as possible to the agent [,] whom he thinks can be fixed.

17

Right: James W. Renton (HSSKC)

Below: First locomotive in Snohomish County, 1883 (HPCUW)

"I am in favor of doing something in order to give us a chance until the next meeting of Congress, when the bill will undoubtedly be repealed, and our day for purchasing cheap land gone forever."

Bribery of government officials was evidently common in the good old days, but the spirit in which this particular bribery was being proposed was something special. Public resources were not going to be quite as easy to pluck as they had always been. A new era was about to begin.

The opportunities for certain kinds of swindling weren't the only things that seemed to be passing into history. The resources themselves were getting scarcer. The forests were still awesome by the standards of today or any other time. There were miles and miles of virgin timber, and the size of some of the trees was staggering. In 1883, Renton wrote to George H. Foster that "if the stick about which you and our Mr. Young had some conversation [really] is twenty inches at the small end and 144 feet long [and] also a nice clean [i.e., knot-free] stick, we will pay you the price asked, viz.: $125."

But the prime trees that could be felled directly into or next to salt water were becoming harder to find. In January of 1884, when Renton was laid up with a bad eye, his stand-in C. W. Young wrote unequivocally, "The timber contiguous to the Sound is nearly exhausted. The part remaining is such as was passed by in past years."

New times were coming, and they called for new methods and investment. The early 1880s saw the beginning of logging railroads. The object would still be to get the logs to tidewater, but now there would be an intermediate step: first get them to the "landings" where they could be loaded onto railroad cars. (They could be dragged to the landings in the old way—by large, hoofed animals—or in the new way—by a stationary steam winch called a "donkey." A couple of men fed the donkey continually with scrap wood. Sparks from the fire started forest fires more frequently than ever. Still, for the first time, the big trees around Puget Sound did not have to be moved by the muscle power of man or beast.) Anyone could drop or drag a log into the water; not just anyone could build or gain access to a railroad. In return for greater capital investment, the big companies would get greater control of the resource.

The new development came with a sense of urgency. In July 1883, Renton wrote to the home office that "as there is another railroad enterprise starting in the Sound and already incorporated, having its terminal points on Puget Sound and Grays Harbor, we find that it is advisable for us to incorporate our road and the sooner the better. The minute we incorporate and definitely locate our line we are safe but unless we do so they may purchase some terminal property near us, locate their line and have a commission appointed to appraise the value of the

Driving the golden spike. Puget Sound now had rail connections to the Midwest (HSSKC)

right-of-way even through our own property. . . . we must make a move soon. . . . Outside of the advantage that we would have over all others (having without doubt the best body of timber in the country) the road would be a paying one." The Port Blakely company had already begun acquiring land around Skookum Bay, north of Olympia, for its rails and the timber to ship over them. At the beginning of 1884, Renton wrote, "We have come to the conclusion that we had better commence operations in Skookum Bay. . . . We have already purchased about three billion feet of timber and think we had better reap the benefit of some of it. We are [now] meeting with some opposition in securing title to [new] timber land and we have enough to run this mill to full capacity for generations to come."

The logging railroads were to make enormous changes in the economic activity around Puget Sound, but changes wrought by the larger roads, the transcontinental lines from the Midwest, were to be much more profound.

The whole economic orientation of the Sound was to change. The rails came west from St. Paul. In 1882, Mark Twain wrote (in *Life on the Mississippi*) that "Saint Paul is a wonderful town. It is put together in solid blocks of honest brick and stone, and has the air of intending to stay. . . . St. Paul's strength lies in her commerce. . . . All the streets are obstructed with building material, and this is being compacted into houses as fast as possible, to make room for more—for other people are anxious to build, as soon as they can get the use of the streets to pile up their bricks and stuff in. . . .

"All that I have said of the newness, briskness, swift progress, wealth, intelligence, fine and substantial architecture and general slash and go and energy of St. Paul will apply to his near neighbor, Minneapolis. . . [where] twenty saw-mills produce two hundred million feet of lumber annually. . . . Sixteen railroads meet in Minneapolis, and sixty-five passenger-trains arrive and depart daily."

This thriving industrial complex in the Midwest was to be the big new market and the big new source of capital for Puget Sound. San Francisco's influence wasn't about to disappear, but new and larger strings were to be pulled from Minneapolis and St. Paul.

A new economic geography was being forged.

instead of prosperity...
stagnation and despair

When Washington became a state in 1889, most of its people lived on or near Puget Sound, where the old distinction between mill towns and real cities still applied. Timber was not just the leading industry: it was bigger than ever and growing steadily. John Muir, having traveled around the Sound, wrote in 1888 that "Puget Sound [is] justly famous the world over for the size and excellence of its timber. . . . Throughout its whole vast extent ships move in safety, and find shelter from every wind that blows, the entire mountain-girt sea forming one grand unrivaled harbor and center for commerce.

"The forest trees press forward to the water around all the winding of the shores in most imposing array, as if they were courting their fate, coming down from the mountains far and near to offer themselves to the axe, thus making the place a perfect paradise for the lumberman. . . .

"The best of the timber has been cut for a distance of eight or ten miles from the water. . . . Most of the young trees have been left, together with the hemlocks and other trees undesirable in kind or in some way defective, so that the neighboring trees appear to have closed over the gaps made by the removal of the larger and better ones, maintaining the general continuity of the forest. . . . the observer coming up the Sound sees not nor hears any thing of [the] fierce storm of steel that is devouring the forests, save perhaps the shriek of some whistle or the columns of smoke that mark the position of the mills. All else seems as serene and unscathed as the silent watching mountains."

Stumps and passed-over trees still stood in the outskirts of even the largest cities. The mill towns were still really just clearings in the forest—albeit, by this time, the second-growth forest. Look at the photographs of the time: in the foreground, tall-masted lumber ships ride at anchor, a forest of wooden masts; behind them and beyond the low wooden piers one sees a scattering of sheds or houses, maybe a portion of The Mill itself, and then a dark backdrop of trees. From this cove in the forest, the ships will fan out to China, Hawaii, Chile, Peru, Australia, San Francisco, New York. The anchorage is deep and sheltered. The trees are close. Nothing more is needed.

J. W. Robinson was the man appointed to take the new state constitution to Washington, D.C., in 1889, and secure from President Benjamin Harrison a formal proclamation of statehood. Thirty years later, he recalled meeting with Harrison, Congressman John. L. Wilson, and Secretary of State James G. Blaine, from the old lumbering state of Maine. Blaine "asked me what was the greatest quantity of merchantable timber I had ever known to be on, say, 160 acres in Washington, and I answered him by saying that in the Land Court I represented a timber claimant as against an agricultural claimant in which the issue was whether the land was chiefly valuable for timber or agriculture, in which the witnesses testified, after examination of the timber, that it contained 36,000,000 feet of first-class merchantable timber, and President Harrison said: 'Well, that much timber could hardly grow on 160 acres,' and Secretary Blaine, with [a] twinkle in his eye, said: 'Mr. President, that would depend upon how high it grew.' "

Such, not unreasonably, was the reputation of the Puget Sound country. By the late 1880s, however, shipments of wheat from eastern Washington were important, too. Coal was still a significant export item. And the salmon fisheries were expanding as fish traps proliferated along the approaches to the Fraser River.

The link to the Midwest had grown stronger, but it was still in its early stages. The Northern Pacific had collected on its enormous federal land grant, and in 1888 unloaded the first big chunk of Washington timberland to the group of Minnesota and Wisconsin lumbermen who established the St. Paul and Tacoma Lumber Company. In the same year the Ryan syndicate of St. Paul provided capital to erect a huge smelter in Tacoma, on the edge of Commencement Bay.

As the terminus of the Northern Pacific, Tacoma was in a position to receive shipments of wheat from eastern Washington, and its ocean commerce reflected that fact. Of eighty-one vessels loading and preparing to load cargo at Sound and British Columbian ports on October 6, 1892, twenty-three were at Tacoma. There were seventeen at Port Blakely, six at Port Gamble, only seven at Seattle, where the cargoes included both lumber and coal. Lumber and coal cargoes were being loaded at Tacoma, too, but there were also ten shiploads of wheat and one of flour bound for the United Kingdom.

The Northern Pacific had made a significant difference, but the ultimate link with the Midwest, the connection that in many ways was to shape the Puget Sound economy more than any other, was still to come. It was, of course, James J. Hill's Great Northern Railroad, which in the fall of 1892 was still being built westward from St. Paul. When Hill began the line, businessmen of Seattle, Everett, and the towns that were to become Bellingham all hoped, based on varying combinations of evidence and self-delusion, that their city would become the terminus of

Much has been made of the rivalry between Seattle and Tacoma for commercial supremacy on Puget Sound. While an intense feeling of rivalry did exist during the final decades of the nineteenth century, it was basically an historical aberration. The coming of the Northern Pacific lifted Tacoma out of the pack and made it briefly a contender for first place. The Klondike gold rush pushed it back out of contention. For roughly nine of the past eleven decades, Seattle seemed the city most likely to prosper.

If Seattle had never gotten a rail line, if the bulk of the gold-rush traffic had gone elsewhere, if various other things had or hadn't happened, the story might have been different. But the fact remains that Tacoma was a serious challenger for only a very few years, and if one weighs those few years against the entire period from the early 1850s to the present, Seattle's ultimate prosperity does not look like one of history's great surprises.

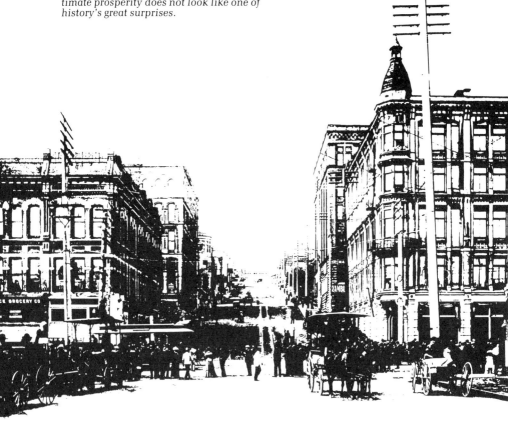

9TH STREET LOOKING FROM A ST., ONE OF THE PRINCIPAL BUSINESS STREETS IN TACOMA.

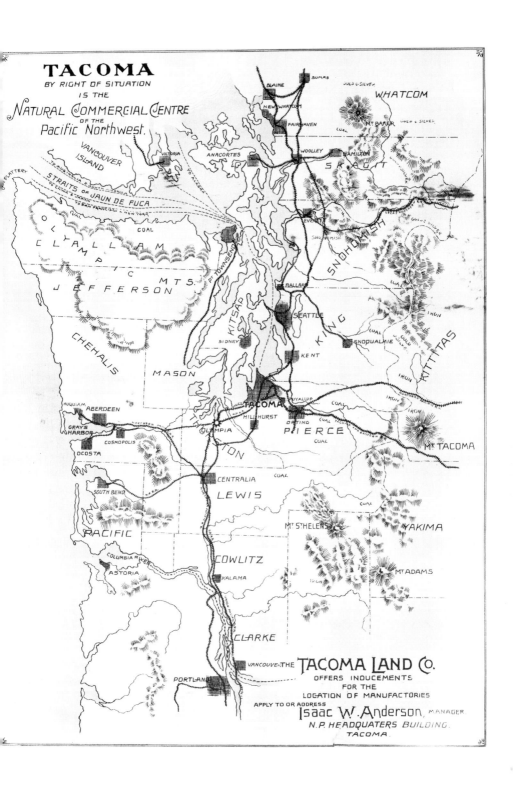

the line. However, Hill envisioned his line as part of an integrated economic network, shipping goods in both directions and linked, at its western terminus, with sea routes to the Orient. Seattle, still the center of regional commerce, with a much more diversified economy than Tacoma or any other city on the Sound, was the logical place. In the fall of 1892, it was clear that Hill would build his line to Seattle.

While the Seattle papers speculated about the completion date of the Great Northern—they thought it would be before the end of 1892, but it wasn't until the following year—neither Seattle nor the Sound in general was stagnating. Even before the line was finished, rails had been laid from Tacoma to Seattle, steamers were running to Alaska from both Seattle and Tacoma, and Hill's Great Northern Steamship Company was advertising regular departures from Seattle to the Orient.

By no means all shipping was bound for places as distant as the Far East or Alaska; virtually all traffic between and among settlements on the Sound still moved by water—and in this local traffic, Seattle still had not only a lead, but a commanding one. The *Seattle Post-Intelligencer's* "Water Front Notes" of September 30, 1892, observed that in Seattle's harbor the "Steamer Fairhaven had thirty tons of potatoes in and fifteen tons of general freight out on the La Conner route; the State of Washington had ten tons out on the Everett route; the Glide took fourteen tons to Tacoma; the Mabel had fifty tons of oats in from Snohomish and took out seventy-two tons of general freight; the J. R. McDonald had sixty-four tons out for Bellingham Bay and the islands; the Yakima came in and took out twenty tons for the Puget Mill Company to Port Gamble; the L. J. Perry had fifty tons of oats in from Snohomish; the Wasco brought in thirty tons of potatoes and left with thirty tons of general freight on the Whatcom route; the Henry Bailey had ten tons in and twenty out on the Skagit River route, and the City of Kingston brought over from Tacoma 1,000 bags of sugar discharged there by the British steamer Victoria."

In the midst of this extensive freight traffic, steamers were carrying passengers among the major and minor cities, halibut schooners were setting out on voyages farther and farther north along the coast of British Columbia, and lumber schooners were carrying more cargo than ever. Port Blakely, still little more than a clearing in the woods on Bainbridge Island, was the lumber ships' largest single port of call. The old Port Blakely Mill had burned down in February 1888. "The fire broke out a few minutes before eight on the morning of the third," Renton wrote. "By 9:50 the mill was a mass of ruins. . . . the fire was caused by a heated journal [the portion of the shaft that joins the bearing] of the small circular engine, and spread so rapidly that some of the men had to jump out of the upper part of the mill." A new mill was soon built, and while it cut less lumber than the St. Paul and Tacoma Lumber

The Hall Brothers shipyard was one of the largest on Puget Sound. There Isaac and Winslow Hall developed the schooner type of lumber carrier (HPCUW, Asahel Curtis photos)

Company's two mills did, it cut more than any other sawmill under one roof.

Next door, the Hall Brothers shipyard, which had begun operation at Utsalady in the 1860s and moved to Port Blakely in 1870, was turning out wooden ships up to 110 feet long. The Sound, despite the success of Hall Brothers and smaller shipyards, despite its excellence as a harbor, despite the large number of boats crossing it daily, entered 1892 as it had entered 1872—with no facilities for repairing large steel ships. If a steamship needed repairs—say a shaft or rudder straightened—and one couldn't or didn't want to take it to San Francisco, one ran her up on the Duwamish flats or some nearby beach and waited for the tide to go out. Naval ships could try the British drydock at Esquimault, British Columbia.

That situation was on the verge of changing. In September, the first floating drydock in the Sound was towed from its building place at Port Hadlock to Dockton, on Vashon Island. Protected from the already sheltered waters of the Sound by the almost encircling land masses of Vashon and Maury Islands, Dockton was as protected a spot as one could possibly find. It was also located on a sparsely settled island with no significant source of materials or labor, but that was less of a handicap in the early 1890s than it was to be a couple of decades later. There was still little overland transportation. Local boats were fueled from stacks of cordwood stored along the shore, and Dockton was no less convenient than almost any place else.

Certainly, it was no less convenient than the future site of Bremerton, on the Kitsap Peninsula, where the U.S. Navy had just decided to build a drydock of its own. In 1888, Congress had authorized the appointment of a commission to choose a site for a navy yard in the Northwest. The senior member of the commission turned out to be Captain Alfred Thayer Mahan, then in the midst of writing a book entitled *The Influence of Sea Power Upon History*. The commission visited the Sound in 1889 and recommended the site that was eventually chosen. There was essentially no labor force and no supplies except raw timber, but both could be shipped easily enough from Seattle. The site itself seemed ideal. In Mahan's words, "It's the citadel of Puget Sound. . . . Within its ample limits not only the Navy but all the merchant shipping of the Sound can find a secure retreat. The situation is upon a good harbor with ample extent and depth of water for ships of the largest size and heaviest draft and is accessible to them at all times."

Congress did nothing but appoint a second commission, which in 1890 agreed with the first. The following year, Congress actually authorized construction of a drydock at "Port Orchard." By then, Mahan, the senior member of the first commission, was well on his way to becoming one of the most influential theorists of his time. His book, which argued that all great nations had exercised control of the seas and that control of the seas was in fact a precondition for greatness, occupied a crucial place in the strategic thinking of the United States and western Europe for the next two decades. It had a particularly powerful effect on the thinking of Theodore Roosevelt and was evidently one of the main reasons why Roosevelt got the United States to start digging a Panama Canal.

In the early 1890s, there was no Canal and no immediate prospect of getting one. The Pacific Ocean was isolated from the major cities of the United States; however it was becoming more important to the country. Japan was developing into a naval power. In the states, there was talk of annexing Hawaii. There was also the territory of Alaska to worry about. There was friction over the treatment of American sailors in Chile. Naval vessels in the Pacific were many weeks away from dry-docks on the East Coast, and since relations between the United States and Britain had never been especially good—they were touchy at best between the War of 1812 and World War I—the U.S. Navy preferred not to rely on the British facilities at Esquimault. On September 30, 1892, the contract for construction of a naval drydock at "Port Orchard" was given to Byron Barlow and Company of Tacoma. The actual construction was to start in December.

Although the Sound was about to get a navy yard and another railroad, although the mills were turning out lumber at a record rate, although the Northern Pacific was bringing wheat across the mountains, and although fisheries and other industries were expanding, there was more than a little economic apprehension and discontent.

Longshoremen and sailors performed brutal work for little money and no job security. Some of those workers had evidently been the target of organizing efforts by the Knights of Labor as early as 1886. In October 1886, Renton wrote that "we had some trouble procuring men for [the vessel] *Kate Davenport*. Mr. Rothschild secured eight at Victoria, and on arriving at Seattle, the Sailors' Union got hold of them. Rothschild had them arrested, and finally we got them aboard ship with deputy sheriffs to watch until [the] vessel was towed out."

The organizing efforts of 1886 soon petered out, but conflicts and discontents along the waterfronts of the Sound did not. There was a lot of discontent throughout the West. The primarily western movement for silver-backed currency—which promised cheaper money for the farmer and a market for the silver from western mines—was gathering strength. Washington was one of the six prosilver western states admitted to the Union in 1889 and 1890. In 1892, for the first time, the prosilver People's Party ran a candidate for President.

The silver movement, like the widespread rural rebelliousness on which it fed, contributed a great deal to the atmosphere of the time, but it had little to offer the workers on ships and docks. There, the issues were a lot more immediate, and they weren't likely to be settled at the polls.

On October 13, 1892, under the headline, "War on the Dock," the *Seattle Post-Intelligencer* carried the story of a confrontation between Seattle longshoremen and Captain Ross of the steamer *Haytian Republic*. Ross assumed, quite accurately, that any able-bodied man could carry cargo off a steamship, and he hated paying longshoremen to do the job. Sometime before, he had tried to get a group of Japanese workers to unload his ship in Seattle, and the longshoremen had had him arrested. This time, when the *Haytian Republic* arrived from Portland around noon, Ross "insisted on his crew handling the freight in the hold of the vessel and letting the longshoremen handle it [only] on the wharf. The longshoremen objected. . . and insisted on doing all the handling or none, so they quit work. The captain then ordered a portion of his crew to go ashore and handle the freight, but the men said they were afraid and refused to obey, whereupon he discharged them. He then tried to induce a number of Chinese passengers. . . to discharge the vessel, but they also were afraid. As a last resort, the captain had a lot of [fishermen] taken down from uptown." After the longshoremen spoke to the fishermen, "they, too, refused to . . . work, some of them yielding to the persuasion of the longshoremen, and others claiming to be afraid, notwithstanding the presence of Chief Jackson and three or four of his officers and patrolmen."

Ross threatened to take his freight back to Portland, but the longshoremen held their ground. Finally, after seven in the evening, a group of shipping-company office workers trucked the freight away "as the captain, steward and the rest of the officers and the cook and waiters on the steamer landed it on the wharf. . . . A number of longshoremen stood away a distance quietly talking among each other and laughing."

The longshoremen had already earned a reputation for toughness and militance. (Not that all their battles were serious; a longshoremen's baseball team played against teamsters and others in the lower Sound.) Confronted with men like Captain Ross, they had little choice. Ross was outraged, but actually, in the context of the times, his labor troubles in Puget Sound were trivial. Working conditions in the heavy industries of the East were brutal beyond anything envisioned on the Sound, management was more aggressive, and labor conflicts, when they arose, were consequently more explosive. In Homestead, Pennsylvania, striking steel workers had just been arrested for treason after fighting pitched gunbattles with an army of Pinkerton guards.

It was not a particularly peaceful time. The newspapers were full of European colonial wars in Africa, the Lizzie Borden ax-murder trial in Boston, the finding of yet another Jack-the-Ripper victim in Glasgow. In Kansas, the Dalton gang rode into Coffeyville and robbed two banks; as the Daltons left town, a small marshall's posse waylaid them and shot them all.

And on Puget Sound, the well-to-do were sailing yachts. Eighteen ninety-two saw the founding of the Seattle Yacht Club. On October 6, the club scheduled a "national regatta." The yachts *Wanda* and *Ripple* sailed down from Fairhaven, on Bellingham Bay, and groups of spectators came by ship from Tacoma and the substantial yachting community at Port Townsend. The yachts were to compete over a course that began and ended at Blakely Rocks, near Port Blakely.

October 6 seemed an auspicious day for Puget Sound in general and Seattle in particular. James J. Hill, having just visited Fairhaven and Everett, gave a little speech in Seattle before his private train pulled out for Tacoma and the Midwest. "I'm not scattering any promises around," said Hill, "but we intend to help develop this section. . . . We propose to develop the lumber business of this region. We not only propose to extend the present market, but also to find new markets for it." The *Post-Intelligencer's* writer observed that "Mr. Hill . . . has already arranged to put handsome steel steamers on the run between here and Alaska next spring. He is also making arrangements to have ocean liners from Puget Sound to China and Japan."

Not even Hill's empire-building speeches could make the wind blow, though, and all the yachts found themselves becalmed. They couldn't sail, much less race, and the regatta was put off until the following day.

The next day, a dense fog covered the Sound. The steamer *Premier* was carrying passengers from New Whatcom to Seattle, blowing her whistle every thirty seconds. Suddenly, off Point No Point, the *Willamette,* carrying twenty-four hundred tons of coal from Seattle to San Francisco, loomed out of the fog. The roughly two dozen passengers in the smoking room heard a crash, started to run, saw the *Willamette's* bow break through into their compartment. At least five people were killed, seventeen injured. The yachts didn't sail.

They didn't sail on the ninth, either.

Finally, on the tenth, in strong winds and rough water, the yachtsmen gave it a try. The Fairhaven yachts *Ripple* and *Wanda* finished first and second. As soon as the *Ripple* completed the course, it capsized. The great international regatta was finally over.

With the growing yachting community; the promise of "handsome steel steamers" to Alaska and the Orient; the constant stream of ships hauling lumber, coal, and wheat to California and around the world; a growing salmon-canning industry; growing lumber mills; a navy yard about to be built; one transcontinental railroad completed and another on the verge of completion, Puget Sound seemed on its way to great prosperity. It wasn't. The completion of Hill's railroad coincided almost exactly with the depression of 1893. Instead of prosperity, the region was entering four years of stagnation and despair.

Top: The Queen, one of the steamers transporting goldmin-
ers from Seattle to the Klondike, 1897 (HSSKC, A.B. Wilse
photo) Middle: Seattle's railroad avenue, 1896 (HSSKC,
A.B. Wilse photo) Bottom: Warships near Bremerton, 1908
(HPCUW, Asahel Curtis photo)

Into the 20th Century

A standard view of the mid-1890s is that for four years, residents of the Puget Sound area reverted to an almost aboriginal lifestyle, combing the beaches and the woods, living on shellfish and berries. Then, on June 17, 1897, the steamer *City of Portland* arrived in Seattle with a ton of gold, touching off the Klondike gold rush, a boom in Puget Sound, Seattle's emergence as the major city on the Sound, and a wave of prosperity that would sweep the region into the twentieth century. That view isn't entirely false, but it is grossly oversimplified.

The gold rush did begin in 1897, Seattle and the rest of the Sound did boom, and the region did start a decade of rapid economic growth. "The great craze for the Klondike is of course quite a help to us in many ways," wrote Chauncey W. Griggs of the St. Paul and Tacoma Lumber Company. He told L. A. Yerkes of Northville, Michigan that "building a steamer for the Tacoma and Whatcom route . . . undoubtedly is a good enterprise and especially will be for business of any kind in our section of the country this coming year, as all of the vessels and old crafts are now engaged with more than they can do. You know the Klondike excitement will put everything that can be floated into use, and in fact some of the boats have made on one trip almost the cost of building them." Seattle wasn't the only city on the Sound that was prospering. "Tacoma . . . is doing more than all the rest of the Sound in importing and exporting products," Griggs wrote hopefully, and he noted that even in Tacoma "property now begins to sell."

Still, Seattle was the city that ultimately profited most. It was the main port from which supplies were shipped north, and it soon dominated the economy of Alaska in the same way San Francisco had long dominated the economy of Puget Sound. Alaska had the raw resources, but Seattle had the home offices, the banks, the suppliers of machinery, the shipping lines. Obviously, no primitive frontier port could have stepped into that role; it required a city with a relatively diversified urban economy. Seattle's ability to cash in on the gold rush was more than a matter of good fortune and energetic self-promotion. The groundwork had been laid for decades. The city had long been the major supplier of logging camps around the Sound, the only Sound port that shipped more general cargo than raw materials. It had also been sending supply ships to Alaska since 1868.

Even in Seattle, the gold rush coincided with a lot of other events. The discovery of gold wasn't the sole cause of prosperity in the late 1890s, or for the social and technological changes of the time. Eighteen ninety-seven happened to be the year the depression ended, not just in Seattle or the Puget Sound region, but all over the country. There was capital for local industry, markets for local products. In September of 1897, Griggs wrote to Yerkes that "we have been running night and day *for the past seven months* [italics added], and lost only seven nights, I think, during that time. Everything in our country seems to be bracing up." A month earlier, he had written to L. B. Royce in Wisconsin that "we in the lumber business here are rushed now beyond anything that has ever occurred before. Orders are piling up upon us and we are obliged to refuse them daily. . . . We have been running three months night and day and have added a 15 horsepower engine to our plant and have just ordered two of the best planers . . . from the east." The letter to Yerkes places the start of prosperity in February. The letter to Royce places it in May. Either way, for the St. Paul and Tacoma Lumber Company, the beginning of a boom in 1897 preceded the arrival of the *City of Portland* by at least a month.

The end of the depression stimulated economic changes throughout the United States. There was a great increase and concentration of business capital, a boom period for the formation of business trusts. "An extraordinary acceleration in the trustification of American industry. . . took place with alarming suddenness in the years from 1898 to 1904," wrote Richard Hofstadter in *The Age of Reform.* "John Moody singles out 1898 as 'the year in which the modern trust-forming period really dates its beginning.' . . . Of the 318 trusts listed by Moody in 1904 . . . 234, with a capitalization of over $6,000,000, had been organized in the years between January 1, 1898 and January 1, 1904."

During that same prosperous decade, the Wright brothers made their first powered flight, and the automobile, which had existed as a novelty in the late 1880s and early 1890s, began insinuating its way into American life. There were 300 cars registered in the United States in 1895, 77,988 by 1905. In 1908, Henry Ford brought out the first mass-produced automobile, the Model T.

The time was prosperous but not entirely peaceful. For both the United States and western Europe, it was a classic period of frank imperialism and military adventure.

Less than a year after the *City of Portland* landed, the United States entered the Spanish American War. Suddenly, the nation had a large military and commercial stake in the Pacific. The whole Sound was a Pacific port. Between 1898 and 1902, the foreign trade of the Washington Customs District doubled. The Bremerton navy yard, which had provided little more than minimal drydock facilities, started getting federal money for expansion in 1900.

For Seattle, 1897 was the first year in which there had been a railroad during a time of prosperity. One might have expected a boom. One couldn't have predicted, though, that the four-year depression would be so good to the railroad's builder, Jim Hill. Hill emerged from the depression with effective control of the Northern Pacific, as well as the Great Northern. The Northern Pacific had been Tacoma's sole means of competing with Seattle for commercial supremacy on the Sound. By the end of the depression, Tacoma still had a railroad of its own, but the road was under Hill's control, and Seattle was the rail terminus that Hill had already chosen.

If Hill was the symbolic railroad builder, the symbolic timber baron of the new century was Hill's St. Paul neighbor, Frederick Weyerhaeuser.

When the depression hit, Weyerhaeuser was already a great timber baron in the Midwest. In 1885, he had turned down the Northern Pacific's offer of timberland and a mill site at Tacoma. By the end of the depression, his view of the Northwest had changed. In 1898, he and his business associates bought into the Coast Lumber Company, a firm that shipped shingles from the Sound to St. Paul. The next year, they bought timber in the Skagit and Sauk River area, near Everett. In 1900, Hill—who was systematically luring midwestern lumbermen to Puget Sound—offered him 900,000 acres of Northern Pacific land-grant timberland at six dollars an acre. Weyerhaeuser and his associates accepted, and the purchase tightened the link between the Sound and the Midwest.

The nineteenth century was the great period of railroad building, but the amount of freight carried by the railroads increased tremendously during the early twentieth century. Concurrently, the Dakotas were being settled and built up, providing a natural, easily accessible market for northwestern lumber. California was still a big lumber market, too, and the rebuilding of San Francisco after the earthquake and fire of 1906 was a bonanza for northwestern mills.

By the time San Francisco burned, Washington was already the leading lumber-producing state in the country, outstripping Mississippi and Louisiana in the Deep South. Most of Washington's production was still coming from the area around the Sound.

More capital, more markets, and better equipment had all helped increase the cut of timber. In the mills, the band saw had become standard equipment. In the woods, the ox team and horse team had largely been replaced by the steam donkey.

Production rose dramatically. Between 1900 and 1905, the mill at Port Gamble increased its cut from 55,642,000 board feet per year to 70,342,000. The Bellingham Bay Improvement Company went from 39,523 to 65,000,000. Port Blakely went from 84,311,000 to 119,231,000.

Left: James Hill (HPCUW)

Sketch: The steam donkey replaced teams of oxen and horses for moving felled trees

Below: Lumber crews relax in bunkhouse (HPCUW, Darius Kinsey photo)

The St. Paul and Tacoma Lumber Company went from 86,378,000 to 125,000,000. In Everett, the Clark-Nickerson Company, which cut 9,000,000 board feet in 1900, cut 50,025,000 in 1905.

As the timber industry grew more substantial, the gap between the way workers were treated and the way they felt they should be treated widened, and some of the workers grew militant. The most militant of all joined the Industrial Workers of the World (I. W. W.), which was founded in 1905 on the premise—the first full sentence in its organizational "manifesto"—that "the working class and the employing class have nothing in common." The I. W. W. found its strongest support in the Puget Sound region, particularly among the men who worked in logging camps. "The I. W. W. movement started in 1905, but it was nearer 1910 when we began to notice slogans painted on stumps along the road: 'I. W. W.,' 'Industrial Workers of the World,' 'One Big Union,' or 'Workers of the World Unite!' " Archie Binns recalled in 1942 in The Roaring Land. "That seemed a strange idea to children, and we wondered what the workers of the world would do after they had united."

Employers didn't wonder; they had visions of disaster. Their concern wasn't confined to the I. W. W. or to the loggers. Workers in all industries were organizing. In 1905, the union locals in Seattle banded together to form a Central Labor Council. In February 1908, the president of the Seattle-based Pacific Coast Steamship Company, J. C. Ford, wrote to Congressman (later Senator) Wesley L. Jones, expressing his concern about a bill being considered by the House Merchant Marine Committee. "Steamship owners . . . look with great suspicion upon a proposed enactment intended to compel them to carry larger crews . . . and defining that each member of such crew shall have had a certain number of years experience at sea," Ford wrote. The bill required at least seventy-five percent of a ship's deck crew to be able seamen and required anyone signed on as an able seaman to have served at least three years on deck at sea or on the Great Lakes.

"There would seem no good reason for crippling our merchant marine by such a provision," Ford wrote. "Take the case of a strike by a Sailors Union. . . . It is well known that the seamen on the Pacific Coast are thoroughly organized into unions. In the event that they . . . should strike, where could those who had 'served three years on deck at sea or on the Great Lakes' be found? . . . the ship owner could do but one of two things: accede to the seamen's demands, or let his vessel rot at the wharf."

Despite the diffuse fears of Ford and other businessmen of the time, the worst capitalist nightmares about organized labor did focus on the logging and mill towns. "At first people did not pay much attention to slogans painted on stumps," Binns wrote, "and then sometimes on week days in good logging weather, towns would be dark and faintly ominous with striking men in stag shirts and overalls."

I. W. W.'s or "wobblies," as they were sometimes called, never succeeded in pulling a majority of the workers around Puget Sound or anywhere else into their "one big industrial union." They didn't win big
strikes, and they didn't build an organization that could last. Within a
decade, though, they convinced Puget Sound employers that more than
half the men in the logging camps were at least sympathetic to I. W. W.
ideas, a prospect that made the employers extremely nervous. The turn
of the century had produced a not always irrational fear of the bomb-
throwing anarchist—an anarchist had assassinated President William
McKinley in 1900. The wobblies stirred up exactly the same sort of fear.

The wobblies themselves were not unhappy to strike fear into the
hearts of the employers who had previously been content to let loggers
sleep with bedbugs in shabby camps. That most logging and milling operations exploited workers was beyond question. It was an exploitive
time, and the forest products industry around Puget Sound was per-
petually insecure. It was far and away the largest industry in the area,
but if one thought of "industry" in terms of brick buildings and big machinery and large capital investment, even the forest products giants
were pretty poor examples of the genre. The company that commanded
the most land and capital, Weyerhaeuser, was content to remain primarily a logging operation, not investing significantly in machinery or
plants until the start of World War I. Some of the other companies pros-
pered; however, competition among them was intense, production often exceeded demand, and many, at best, scraped by.

Even the largest might have been lost without the cheap
transportation to both mills and markets provided by the Sound. The
rail link to the Midwest was all well and good, but rail transportation
was expensive, and by no means all the lumber produced in the Northwest could be shipped by rail and sold at a profit. Major Chauncey
Griggs of the St. Paul and Tacoma Lumber Company said in 1924 that
since the company started operations in 1889, it had never been able to
make money shipping any but the very best lumber by rail. To sell
enough common lumber to keep its mills going, the company had had
to enter markets that could be reached by ship.

Griggs and the other mill owners looked not simply to ships, but to
cheap ships. They weren't especially interested in the building of a
modern merchant marine. What they really wanted were old tubs just
sound enough to take a load of lumber down the coast. The moderniza-
tion of American shipping was the last thing that interested them. In
1908, an official of the Stimson Mill Company in Ballard wrote to Wesley L. Jones, "We are advised that there is a bill before Congress, known
as the Gallinger Amendment to the Shipping Act of March 3rd, 1891,
providing for a subsidy of $4.00 for steamships of sixteen knots and up-
wards for carrying the mail between the United States and South
American and the United States and Asiatic points.

"The present law requires a speed of twenty knots to secure this subsidy and it works a great hardship on the slower speed vessels, which are a majority of the present vessels engaged in the [lumber] trade."

Lumber went on the slow steamships, and it still went on sailing vessels, too. Puget Sound was the last place in the United States where sailing vessels were used extensively to carry cargo. The reason was not that the people who lived around Puget Sound were particularly fond of the picturesque but that sailing vessels were a cheap way to move lumber out of the Sound.

Most port communities around the Sound shipped lumber and little else, but for the Sound as a whole, it wasn't the only cargo. For Seattle, which handled roughly eighty percent of the Washington Customs District's foreign trade, it was a minor part of the traffic. Both Seattle and Tacoma were still shipping large amounts of flour and wheat. The main cargo shipped from Seattle was general merchandise. Supplies of all kinds were going to Alaska, and fish, furs, and gold were coming back.

Virtually everything that traveled between towns on Puget Sound still went by ship. The "mosquito fleet" of small passenger ships still tied together all the cities and towns around the Sound. Although wood was still ubiquitous and coal plentiful, the turn of the century saw most of the fleet converting to oil for fuel. It also saw regular service extended to more and more communities. Every little settlement had its own pier. Roads between even nearby communities were few and mostly primitive.

"The only means of transportation on Hood Canal was by boat," Captain Torger Birkland recalled in the 1970s, for a *History of Kitsap County*. "Instead of building docks, every [logging] camp had a raft anchored out in deep water where the steamer would land.

"The *Perdita* was the first passenger and freight boat that I saw on this body of water. She came in to our camp about twice a week with canned goods and fresh meat. This was usually at the noon hour. . . . [It] was looked forward to by all hands.

"Camps where horses were used for hauling logs (which was the most common at that time) received the bulk of the ship's cargo, such as baled hay and oats for feed and large wooden stave barrels of crude oil used for greasing the skids. These barrels were usually rolled out through the port and overboard to be picked up by the boom man and towed to the beach by him. . . .

"About 1905 the steamer *Inland Flyer* came on the run. . . . This boat had just then been converted from coal to oil and was the first in the 'Mosquito Fleet' to burn oil."

Top: The H.B. Kennedy, one of the passenger ships that tied together the cities and towns around Puget Sound. Below: The "mosquito fleet" at Coleman Dock in Seattle (PSMHS/WC, Webster & Stevens)

By steamboat or rowboat, one could easily reach virtually any place on the Sound. As the cities grew, prosperous city dwellers began building summer dwellings in underdeveloped, but easily accessible, spots on the Kitsap Peninsula and on Vashon and other islands. During the very first years of the century, clumps of small summer houses were springing up in remote locations all around the rim of the lower Sound.

It was easy enough for any of those straw-hatted, turn-of-the-century vacationers or for any logger or mill hand on his day off to drop a line into the waters of the Sound and catch fish for his own consumption. Commercial fishing was a much different story. To catch halibut commercially, for example, men sailed hundreds of miles from Puget Sound on large schooners. The halibut fishery had started in 1888; the winter before, three schooners set sail from Gloucester and Swampscott, Massachusetts, sailed around the Horn and came to the Sound to catch halibut in the traditional Makah Indian fishing ground near the mouth of the Strait of Juan de Fuca. The boats originally made their headquarters at Port Townsend, close to the fishing ground. It proved a bad choice. Port Townsend was separated by the entire length and width of the Sound from Tacoma, where the fish were iced and shipped eastward on the Northern Pacific. The costs of icing and shipping were very high during the first few years of the halibut fishery, and the added awkwardness of operating from Port Townsend proved too much. The halibut fleet soon moved to Seattle. Subsequently, New England companies based other halibut boats in Tacoma and in Vancouver, British Columbia. The boats continued to use the Sound as a home port, but as the halibut stocks were depleted, the skippers began sailing farther and farther north along the B.C. coast. By the turn of the century, they were pushing into the hazardous waters off Alaska. And they were still sailing big schooners, not boats most individual fishermen could reasonably dream of owning.

Small boats were used to catch salmon commercially, but the small-boat fisherman was not the backbone of the industry; to catch large numbers of salmon, the big canning companies still relied primarily on fish traps.

To process those salmon, one sought the cheapest possible labor. Throughout the late nineteenth century, at canneries all along the Pacific Coast, from the Sacramento River to Alaska, the work of cleaning and packing salmon was done by Chinese laborers who did the work quickly and thoroughly for very little pay. Cannery work was known as the sort of labor that "no white man would do."

It was a time of mechanization, though, and given a choice between even cheap human labor and a machine, one chose a machine. In 1903, a machine that headed and gutted salmon automatically was installed in the Pacific American Fisheries' cannery in Bellingham. With

Right: The Iron Chink (HPCUW, Asahel Curtis photo) Below: Around the turn of the century, purse seining for salmon was a labor intensive endeavor. Few boats had gasoline engines, and nets were hauled by hand. San Juans 1905 (WMHA).

the unselfconscious racism of the time, the machine—which replaced so many Chinese workers—was christened the "iron chink." It is still called the iron chink. Soon, the machine was being used in canneries all along the coast, increasing production and the major canning companies' appetite for fish.

The same wave of technological progress that increased efficiency in the canneries soon increased the efficiency of the small fishing boat. The position of the small fisherman changed rapidly. One fisherman who experienced the change was Phil Green, first of what by the late 1970s were three generations of commercial salmon fishermen. Green's father's family came west by covered wagon sometime in the 1880s. For some reason, the family had already decided to seek its fortune on the shores of Hood Canal, where the Pope & Talbot mills were operating full bore. The Greens camped for four months in a part of what is now downtown Seattle, building a boat. When the boat was finished, they sailed around the tip of the Kitsap Peninsula to Hood Canal, where they homesteaded. Farmers did not generally prosper on the shores of Hood Canal. The only real source of money was the logging and milling operations, where the Green men could and did earn ten cents an hour for a ten-hour day.

As Green's son, himself a purse seiner for forty-eight years, recalls the family history, one could catch salmon in Hood Canal, but there was no place to sell them. There were no canneries or salteries nearby, nowhere one could be sure of selling the fish before they spoiled. Then regular steamer service began to Seattle. (The ship may have been the same *Perdita* that Captain Birkland recalled.) Green and other young men began catching salmon just in time for the steamer to take them to Seattle and sell them to restaurants.

In 1905 or a little before, Green started rowing up to the salmon banks off the San Juan Islands to take a crack at the Fraser River fish. He and the men who rowed with him from Hood Canal were purse seiners. They fished from two four-man, flat-bottomed skiffs. Each skiff would take one end of a net. One of the skiffs would remain stationary and the other would swing out around a school of fish, surrounding them. The Hood Canal men were among the first fishermen to work the salmon banks from small boats, but they weren't the very first. Others before them had rowed out from Bellingham and all the way up from Gig Harbor. In the San Juans, the fishermen would all camp on the beach, and whenever possible, get a passing steam tug to pull them out to the fishing grounds. There were three distinct camps. The Scandinavians set up their camp on Lopez Island. The "Austrians"—that is, the Slavs whose homeland was still part of the Austro-Hungarian Empire—set up theirs on San Juan Island. Green and others, who were neither Scandinavian nor Slavic, camped in a different spot on San Juan.

They did this for several years during which nets were pulled straight from the water by hand and the only reliable source of power—other than the occasional passing tug—was a set of nine-foot oars. But the technology of purse seining soon changed. Around 1909, Phil Green decided it was inefficient to haul the nets bodily over the sides of the boats and rigged his own boats with masts and booms so that the nets could be raised by men pulling down on ropes run through pulleys. The mast and boom quickly became standard equipment.

Around the same time, the nine-foot oar was giving way to the gasoline engine. The first motorized purse seiner appeared off Point No Point in the summer of 1903—exactly the same fishing season, incidentally, that saw the introduction of the iron chink. During the next decade, virtually all the fishermen put gas motors in their boats. Green got his in 1909. It was a two-cylinder engine that overheated if both cylinders were used. Standard procedure was to connect only one spark plug for routine cruising. If a school of fish was sighted, Green would hook up the second cylinder for the chase. As soon as the chase was over, he would disconnect it.

Those first gasoline engines were crude and dangerous—a gasoline fire made short work of a small wooden boat—but they revolutionized fishing and enabled Americans to catch an even larger share of the Fraser River runs. They also turned the Slavic or Scandinavian or Anglo-Saxon fisherman into a small businessman. It was one thing to own a couple of rowboats, quite another to own, say, a thirty-footer that could go anywhere in the Sound under its own power.

The gasoline engine had a similar, perhaps a greater, impact on the halibut fishery. The old schooners that went all the way to Alaska powered by nothing but sail were big ships that required big crews and lots of capital. The immigrant fisherman might work on one as a crew member, but he was in no position to own one. Ownership was reserved primarily for Yankee businessmen and corporations.

The introduction of gasoline motors in the decade before World War I changed all that. One no longer needed a full-rigged sailing ship or a steamer with a commensurate crew. The immigrant—not every immigrant, to be sure, but the sea-going immigrant entrepreneur—could get an efficient boat of his own. By the start of World War I virtually all the schooners had gasoline engines, at least for auxiliary power. Crews ranged anywhere from five to seventy-five men. Most of the boats had Scandinavian owners. Owners of vessels in the Puget Sound halibut fleet at the beginning of 1914 included Larsen, Nelsen, Lindvog, Hansen, Nilsen, Tonneson, Knutsen, Johansen, Endresen, and others of obviously Scandinavian origin.

The internal combustion engine democratized water transportation, just as the car and truck democratized transportation on land, freeing people from their dependence on giant railroad companies as the only alternative to the horse. The gas engine did cost more than a pair of oars, but it gave individual fishermen a mobility, a rapidity of movement that only businesses large enough to operate steamers or sailing ships had commanded before.

Once individual fishermen owned their own motorized and potentially profitable boats for catching salmon or halibut, they began to set up small communities around the rim of the Sound at places like Poulsbo and Colby and Olalla on the Kitsap Peninsula, and on Vashon and the San Juan Islands. There were plenty of coves that offered secure, protected moorages for their boats. They could farm or take other jobs when they weren't fishing. They could sell salmon to a fish market or cannery just about any place around the Sound, although the major buyers were concentrated in the major cities. John Cobb, the editor of *Pacific Fisherman* and later dean of the University of Washington College of Fisheries, wrote in 1914 that "fresh fish is landed and sold wherever there is a hamlet of any size in Puget Sound. The major part of the products, however, are landed at Seattle, Tacoma and Everett." If a fisherman didn't want to go all the way into port, he could load his catch onto one of the many steamers following regular schedules across the Sound. If he was catching halibut off Alaska, he could ship his catch by steamer from there. In the northern Sound particularly, one could deliver salmon to a cannery just about anywhere; Everett, Anacortes, Port Townsend, Port Angeles, Bellingham, Blaine, Friday Harbor, and other towns all had canneries large or small.

Did anyone worry about the survival of the fish? There is little evidence that anyone worried very much. True, as closer halibut populations were wiped out, the halibut fishermen had pushed their way farther and farther north to find enough fish. True, ever since territorial days, Washington had imposed some restrictions—seldom honored or even enforced—on fishing times and fishing gear for salmon. True, small dams were already cutting some populations of salmon off from their spawning grounds. But in general, there was little awareness of, much less concern about, depletion of the resources.

If anything, the atmosphere was one of self-congratulation. Nineteen-thirteen was a record year for Fraser River salmon, the largest catch and largest cannery pack ever recorded. "The total pack in 1913 amounted to 2,583,463 cases of all species, with a market value of $13,-329,168, a sum almost as great as the value of the gold brought this year from all Alaska," observed the 1914 *Pacific Fisherman Yearbook*. "The greater part of the catch of the Puget Sound fisherman is made from [the Fraser River] run. . . . Extensive as are the operations of the industry, they do not necessitate the annihilation or reduction of the great wealth which the waters hold. Nor does it mean the confiscation of a public

Top: Gasoline engines revolutionized Puget Sound fishing.
Below: Spring 1914. Trying to clear the 1913 rockslide that
impeded Fraser River salmon runs (HPCUW, Cobb photos)

resource for private profit. The salmon canning industry on Puget Sound will be 40 years old next year, yet the pack of canned salmon for 1913 is greater than that of any year on record."

The Canadians had been arguing for nearly two decades that the Fraser River salmon were actually in trouble. Canadians had been canning Fraser River salmon since 1870 and had been fishing for them longer than that. It is possible that they were truly concerned about the survival of the runs. It is certain that they did not like seeing American fish traps and American seiners taking two-thirds of the fish from their rivers. Nor could they have liked the settlement of their boundary with southeast Alaska, farther up the same coast. The original Anglo-Russian treaty of 1825 had fixed the boundary of southeast Alaska as a line parallel to the coast and ten marine leagues inland. Beginning in 1888, Canada claimed the inland measurement should begin not on the coast of the mainland, but at the outermost points of the outermost islands. In 1903, the Alaskan Boundary Tribunal, in London, ruled against the Canadian claim. That must have made the American capture of so many fish from western Canada all the more galling.

In 1908, Canada and the United States established a commission to study the condition of the Fraser River runs and to make recommendations about their management. The next year, the commission recommended regulation of both fish traps and boats and a two-day closed period during every week of the fishing season. Canada was willing to put the recommendations into practice immediately. The United States was not. The big canning companies in Puget Sound were already processing the bulk of the Fraser River fish, and they didn't want any regulations that would give them a smaller share. The Washington State congressional delegation did not customarily oppose the canning industry. Congress as a whole deferred to the Washington delegation on a matter of regional interest. The agreement was never signed.

Right after the record season of 1913, though, the Fraser River situation changed dramatically. The Canadian Pacific was building a railroad through Hells Gate, roughly one hundred miles northeast of Vancouver. Crews were using dynamite to blast a path through the rock. One blast touched off a huge rockslide, which tumbled down into the Fraser River, blocking most of the channel that the sockeye used to reach their spawning grounds. Canada may have been shedding crocodile tears over the sockeye before, but now it was clear that the fish were genuinely in trouble.

*Right: Logging truck,
1918 (HPCUW)*

*Below: World War I
created a demand for the
Sound's harbors and ship-
building sites (HSSKC,
Webster & Stevens)*

the automobile
commenced to dig in

Nineteen-fourteen was a turning point for more than the Fraser River salmon. It also marked the beginning of World War I. On Puget Sound, as elsewhere, the war years saw a profound shift in social and economic patterns. They were the break with the nineteenth century, the beginning of the end of the good old days.

The war also brought a quick end to the bad old days that had followed the economic slump of 1909 and 1910. The economy of the whole country had taken a turn for the worse at that point, and the markets for Puget Sound lumber had contracted. The mills were still grinding out more lumber than was produced any place else in the country, but in fact, they were grinding out too much: with hundreds of mills and a glut of lumber, it was hard for anyone to make a profit. Many mills closed. Since most of the jobs in the Puget Sound area were connected with cutting trees or milling lumber or shingles, times weren't good. The radical I. W. W. grew stronger, spreading apprehension among employers.

The world war and the United States' eventual involvement in it changed all that. The market for lumber picked up. The big timber and milling companies made money hand over fist. On the Olympic Peninsula, the federal government set up an operation to cut and process spruce for aircraft construction. The man in charge of the federal operation, Colonel Disque, set up the Loyal Legion of Loggers and Lumbermen as an alternative to the wobblies, who had made what turned out—in the superpatriotic atmosphere of wartime—to be a fatal mistake by starting a strike in the lumber industry. The I. W. W. lost most of its support.

The war created a demand for both lumber and fish. More importantly, it increased the demands for the Sound's harbors and shipbuilding sites.

All other things being equal, Puget Sound had always been an ideal place in which to load, unload, build, repair or launch ships. But all other things had seldom been equal. The Sound provided a fine geographical setting for shipbuilding, but it had always been far from major markets, far from any raw materials except wood and coal, far from supplies of skilled labor. It had always been cheaper to build ships elsewhere, more profitable to unload most cargoes closer to major population centers.

Even before the war, there seemed a chance that this situation would change. For years, every seaport on the Pacific Coast had been looking forward to the opening of the Panama Canal, which would make the East Coast and Europe weeks closer. Piers were lengthened and harbors dredged. The Canal was completed in 1914, just in time for the war. The Canal carried very little merchant shipping throughout the war years and had very little direct impact on Puget Sound or other West Coast ports. The war itself did have an impact. With German submarines roaming the Atlantic and many European supplies cut off by the war, oriental goods and Pacific ports grew more important. All the Sound ports were busy, and Seattle became one of the leading ports in the country. By 1918, Puget Sound was handling more cargo than any American port except New York, more trade with the Orient than any other port in the United States.

The boom in shipbuilding was even more striking. The United States had long relied on foreign merchant ships to carry most of its cargo. Foreign crews—even northern European and British crews—received less pay and tolerated poorer living conditions than did U.S. crews, so the ships of their nations were cheaper to operate. When the war began, though, the European countries needed their ships, and German submarines were blowing them out of the water at an alarming rate. Even before the United States entered the war, the nation's merchant fleet simply didn't have enough vessels to meet the shippers' needs.

The federal government consequently swept aside a couple of long-standing policies for the duration of the war. It allowed foreign ships—if any were available—to carry cargoes between U.S. ports. And it began financing the building of ships. In 1916, Congress authorized the establishment of a U.S. Shipping Board to regulate the American merchant marine and promote the construction of ships and shipyards. The Board and its ship-financing subsidiary, the Emergency Fleet Corporation, went to work after the United States entered the war in 1917. The goal was to get the largest possible number of merchant ships built in the shortest possible time. The E. F. C. paid for ships built of wood as well as steel. Money was no object. Shipyards all around the Sound had orders. New yards sprang up. Seattle became a great shipbuilding center, with five yards for steel ships and a dozen for wooden ones. Workers came to the shipyards from all over the inland West. For once, the Sound had a major industry that did not consist primarily of handling raw materials with the lowest possible labor cost. Government contracts assured the shipyard owners of a profit. All they had to do was get their ships built. To do that, they needed workers. They lured workers from all over, even from other West Coast shipyards, with the highest wage scale in the country. The workers came. The Boilermakers' local in Seattle claimed to be the biggest single union local in the world.

The war fueled a short-term economic binge—inherently temporary, inherently different from what came before or would come afterward. When it ended, the Puget Sound area had to go through a difficult period of adjustment. For some people, it was necessary to accept the fact that things would not continue to be as they had been during the war. For others, it was necessary to accept the fact that wartime changes were going to last.

The shipyard boom did not, could not, survive the armistice. With the war over, there was an instant surplus of ships. The government had no reason to finance more construction. There would be no market for privately financed vessels. The yards got ready to close.

Many of the men who had come from other parts of the West to work in Puget Sound shipyards prepared to move on—to a shingle mill in Oregon, a homestead in Wyoming, or elsewhere. Others tried to turn back the clock. Before the war ended, the federal government had placed a lid on the wages that could be paid workers in the Puget Sound shipyards. If the employers paid more, the government would not reimburse them for the extra wages. With the war coming to an end, the employers had no incentive to stretch the government guidelines. The shipyard unions appealed to the federal Labor Adjustment Board, but lost. Early in the war, the unions might have been able to force the employers to pay the workers what they wanted. Late in the war, their chances were slim. When the war ended, they had no chance at all. Nevertheless, within a month after the armistice, the shipyard workers voted to strike. Early in 1919, the other unions in the Seattle Central Labor Council voted to join them. The first general strike in American history was born.

There have been many different analyses of motives for, and the events leading to, the Seattle general strike of February 1919—which proved to be an eight day model of orderliness and futility—but the main underlying motive seems clear: the unions wanted to forestall the inevitable, to hang onto the jobs and wage levels that Seattle's shipyard economy had supported during the war. "They had nothing to lose," a Puget Sound labor radical of the time, Jack Miller, told Los Angeles writer Mary Deaton nearly sixty years later. "If they didn't strike, the shipyards would close anyway. It was an act of desperation."

The general strike was the last significant flare-up of labor radicalism on Puget Sound until the 1930s. During the war, when jobs were plentiful and labor scarce, organized workers, not only in the shipyards, but also on steamboats and elsewhere, had grown very assertive. Now, jobs were suddenly scarce, and servicemen were coming home to

Left: Shipbuilding boomed on Puget Sound during World War I (HPCUW, Asahel Curtis photo)

Below: Despite appeals from the press, the first general strike in American history took place in February 1919 (HPCUW)

U. S. OFFICERS TO DISCUSS STRIKE

—SEE PAGE 2

FULL Leased Wire of the United Press Association.

COMPLETE Service of the Newspaper Enterprise Association.

The Seattle Star

FINAL EDITION

TWO CENTS IN SEATTLE

THE GREATEST DAILY CIRCULATION OF ANY PAPER IN THE PACIFIC NORTHWEST

VOLUME 21. NO. 290

SEATTLE, WASH., TUESDAY, FEBRUARY 4, 1919.

Weather Forecast: Tonight and Wednesday, probably rain; strong gales tonight, decreasing tonight and Wednesday

STOP BEFORE IT'S TOO LATE

This is plain talk to the common-sense union men of Seattle. You are being rushed pell-mell into a general strike. You are being urged to use a dangerous weapon—the general strike, which you have never used before—which, in fact, has never been used anywhere in the United States. It isn't too late to avert the tragic results that are sure to come from its use.

You men know better than any one else that public sentiment in Seattle—that is, the sentiment of the ninety per cent of the people who are not directly involved in the wage dispute of the shipworkers—*is against a general strike*. You know that the general public doesn't think the situation demands the use of that drastic, disaster-breeding move. *You know, too, that you cannot club public sentiment into line, and you know, too, that no strike has ever been won without the moral support of the public.*

The people know that there is a decent solution of the issue at stake. And the issue at stake is merely a better wage to the average unskilled worker in the shipyards. To a large extent public opinion is with these unskilled workers now, but public opinion will turn against them if their wage issue brings chaos and disaster upon the whole community unnecessarily. Seattle today is awake to the fact that she is on the brink of a disaster, *and Seattle is getting fighting mad.* The people are beginning to visualize the horrors that a general tie-up will bring. They see the suffering that is bound to come and *they don't propose to be silent sufferers.*

Today Seattle resents this whole miserable mess. Seattle resents the insolent attitude of the shipyard owners; Seattle resents the verbosity of Director General Piez, whose explanation does not explain, and just as emphatically resents the high-handed "rule or ruin" tactics of the labor leaders who propose to lay the whole city prostrate in a vain attempt to show their power. Let us not mince words. A general strike cannot win unless one of two things happens. Either the ship owners and Piez must yield or else the workers must be able to control the situation by *force*. The latter method no doubt would be welcomed by the agitators and the babblers of Bolshevikism. But the latter method is bound to be squelched without much ado, and you decent union men of Seattle will be the sufferers then. *A revolt--and some of your leaders are talking of a revolution--*to be successful must have a country-wide application. There isn't a chance to spread it east of the mountains. There isn't a chance to spread it south of Tacoma *and today fifty per cent of the unions of Tacoma have turned down the proposition for a general strike.*

Confined to Seattle or even confined to the whole Pacific coast, the use of force by Bolsheviks would be, and should be, quickly dealt with by the army of the United States. These false Bolshevik leaders haven't a chance on earth to win anything for you in this country, *because this country is America--not Russia.*

compete for them. Smart employers realized that times were changing, that the local labor force would have to be a lot more manageable in the future. Joshua Green, whose Puget Sound Navigation Company ran steamboats all over the Sound, wrote on February 27, 1919 that "fire-brick, when they are not crated, seem to get our deck hands' goats. . . . we simply can't keep crews and make them handle fire-brick. . . . we had 2,000 brick lay on our dock a month for Victoria; every time we told our crews to load them they quit, and we simply had to put in [a] crat[ing] rule." Green noted, however, that "I think pretty soon we can drop that rule, as labor is getting more reasonable every day."

Organized workers in the shipyards and on ships weren't the only people who would have been happy to turn back the clock. Leaders of the shipping and shipbuilding industries, who had done so well during the war and were now faced with a return of the cheaper foreign competition, were also eager to hang onto their wartime gains. Unlike the blue-collar workers, they had a powerful ally: Washington's senior senator, Wesley L. Jones, the chairman of the Senate Commerce Committee.

The United States emerged from the armistice with a huge new merchant fleet, a new government bureaucracy to supervise it, an unfulfilled desire for a great privately owned merchant marine, and no post-war shipping policy. No one was in a better position to create a national shipping policy than Jones. Early in 1920, his committee came up with a bill that would establish a loan fund to help finance private shipbuilding, discriminate heavily against foreign shipping wherever possible, and create a new federal shipping board. Only American ships were to be allowed to carry cargo between American coastal ports, or between the forty-eight states and any of the United States' island possessions or Alaska. In addition, preferential rail rates were to be given cargoes destined for American ships. Jones rammed the bill through, virtually without discussion. The bill—known ever since as the Jones Act—was "one of the most important measures on shipping ever brought before Congress," wrote Paul Maxwell Geiss eighteen years later in his study of American Shipping Policy, yet it "received practically no debate in the Senate and passed without a record vote. . . . Its real parents were not the Senate and the House of Representatives but rather the Senate Commerce Committee and the shipping lobby."

There is no evidence that Jones was acting in direct response to the shipping lobby, but there is no reason to doubt it. He had long lent a sympathetic ear to the problems of J. C. Ford and other shipping executives, and he could scarcely have been oblivious to the impact that the end of the war had had on shipping and shipbuilding in his own home state.

Jones himself didn't deign to justify or explain the Act publicly until August, when, with an election coming up in the fall, he returned to Washington State to talk with his constituents. One of his stops was the Tacoma Commercial Club, where what *The New York Times* called the largest gathering of shipping and port men ever held on the West Coast had assembled for a luncheon and a discussion of the Jones Act. Not all of Jones's constituents had been pleased by the legislation. Far from it. Port officials feared that by discriminating against foreign shipping, the Act would simply drive foreign ships north of the border to Vancouver, British Columbia. Given a choice between the shipping interests and the ports, a Seattle port commissioner complained, Jones had chosen the shippers.

Jones faced the shippers and angry port men on a hot day in a crowded room. He gave a prepared speech, had lunch, then beat a judicious retreat, leaving a representative, W. C. Clark, to answer questions. Clark was, not just coincidentally, the president of the Pacific Steamship Company. He pointed out, among other things, that since merchant ships had begun using the Panama Canal, the West Coast had already lost a lot of oriental cargoes; the Jones Act wasn't responsible for the cargo loss. The port officials weren't convinced. "At times, the scene resembled almost a riot," *The New York Times* reported. "Businessmen in their shirt sleeves, because of the great heat . . . rose in anger at statements which Mr. Clark made."

In his morning speech to the group, Jones had said that "when the war came, we had only a little more than 1,000,000 tons of shipping in the foreign trade. Now we have under construction in private yards more than 1,300,000 tons." He made it clear that his legislation was designed to keep the shipyards busy and to maintain the wartime momentum toward a big American merchant fleet. He also said that the most controversial portion of the Act had been suggested by the U.S. Shipping Board. A few days before the hot, angry meeting in Tacoma, the chairman of the Shipping Board, Admiral W. S. Bensen, had justified the Board's position in a letter to Seattle port commissioner, W. T. Christiansen. Bensen had told Christiansen that "there apparently has not entered into your calculations the fact that unless American ships be substituted for foreign ships in the carrying of the greater part of your Oriental commerce, the shipyards of the Puget Sound, which have given employment to many thousands of workmen, bringing abundant prosperity to your community, must close their gates."

The Jones Act was no more successful than the general strike had been. Most shipyards closed their gates anyway. Foreign ships were still cheaper to operate than American vessels, and as the foreign shipping nations rebuilt their fleets after the war, the foreign ships became faster and more efficient, too.

Foreign trade through the Washington Customs District, which had more than quintupled between 1914 and 1919, plunged abruptly and didn't regain its wartime volume for decades. The great trade in Japanese soybean oil that had developed during the war was soon cut off by a prohibitive American tariff.

Puget Sound's natural advantages as a shipbuilding center and harbor still couldn't compensate entirely for its remote location. The Northwest had not moved closer to the population centers of the East.

Around the Sound itself, the western and eastern shores were in a sense moving farther apart. The patterns and economics of local transportation were starting to change. The water was still filled with boats, but people no longer felt that the boats were enough.

Vashon, totally dependent on water transportation, offers a good example: the water around Vashon was as full of activity as ever. Sternwheelers were unloading bales of hay and straw at little local docks, two enterprising men were launching their own gasoline-powered freight boat, a special steamer was taking men to the surviving Tacoma shipyards every morning, the schooner *Anne J. Larson* was bringing in halibut, the *Bud* was being remodeled as a salmon troller, the *Fisher Boy* was heading for the salmon banks off the San Juans with an eight-man crew, and the local shipyards were overhauling fishing schooners and launches and repairing steamers. On a rainy Saturday morning, the brand-new Martinolich yard launched its first vessel, the 250-foot *Dockton*.

Despite all this activity, the only maritime event that rated front-page headlines in the local paper was the establishment of direct ferry service to Seattle. The ferry would follow a less leisurely schedule than the Seattle and Tacoma steamers that called regularly at docks around the island. More important, it would carry cars and trucks. "A New Era for Vashon Island Ushered in by Ferry," said the headlines.

A new era had already arrived. Captain Birkland, who became second mate of the steel steamer *Potlatch* in 1917, recalled the change six decades later for a *History of Kitsap County* and began by reciting the route the steamer had followed between Seattle and the small towns on Hood Canal. "At 9 A.M. we took our departure from Seattle," he said, "stopped at Maxwelton and Austin on Whidbey Island. From there, across Admiralty Inlet to Port Ludlow, then to Port Gamble, then Lofall and Bangor about noon and also some logging camp stops in between.

"From Bangor to Hazel Point and Coyle, then to Seabeck and then across to Brinnon. From Brinnon to Duckabush where the old fellow came out to meet us with his big rowboat.

"From there to Triton's Cove and across to Nellita along the shore to Holly and to the peninsula side again to Eldon and the Hamma Hamma [near Crawford and Nelson's logging camp]. . . . Dewatto, Lil-

*Hauling logs out of the woods on a trestle road
(HPCUW, Darius Kinsey photo)*

liwaup, Hoodsport and Potlatch. Before arrival at Union City, the end of the long run, arriving there around 6:30 P.M., departing Union 7:00 for the return trip, making numerous stops to take on loggers and, during vacation season, people were on the move with camping gear and fishing outfits. . . .

"In late fall, 1917, the service of this fine little ship . . . came to an end on Hood Canal. Roads had been completed pretty well around from Shelton, and also a narrow road to Bremerton. So here the automobile commenced to dig in and take its toll."

The automobile had really caught on during the war. Paved roads were being built to accommodate it. Trucks were being used to haul logs out of the woods. The Everett Commercial Club sent out messages on letterhead that not only proclaimed Everett the "greatest lumber and shingle center in the United States," but also boasted that "Snohomish County is spending over $2,000,000 for a complete system of permanent cement highways." Everett had had telephones for more than twenty-five years; a network of paved highways was something new.

Finally, it was becoming as quick and easy to travel on land as on the water. Highways didn't cost anything to use, either. In the meantime, the costs of running boats had gone up; it no longer seemed quite as cheap to serve a small community as not to serve it. Boat service had been cut back somewhat during the war. In many cases, it was not restored. Places that had relied on the service to be tied into the economic and social life of the Sound now found themselves cut off.

One such place was the former center of the lumber industry, the mill town par excellence, Port Gamble. Port Gamble hadn't been the center of the industry for a long time, but it had been in the mainstream; suddenly, it was peripheral. The post-war letters of Pope & Talbot's manager there, Edwin G. Ames, reflect a frustration with the new order of things and suggest that Ames—like Senator Wesley Jones and the Seattle strikers—wanted nothing more or less than to turn back the clock.

In April 1919, Ames wrote to Nels Sonju, who had a government contract to carry mail overland from Poulsbo to the Pope & Talbot mill towns, that "I have looked into the matter of change in the mail service and . . . would say that we are not satisfied with the existing arrangement at all. We were better served by the water routes, making mail deliveries at Gamble and Ludlow by steamer, than we have been by the more complicated system of service which has been and is now being rendered. We are interested in the steamboat service. . . and have been trying to get at least one of these water routes restored. . . . We have no particular interest in stage routes, auto lines or anything of that nature . . . . We are interested in getting a good steamboat service between our mills at Port Gamble and Port Ludlow and Seattle."

Two months earlier, in a tone both more irate and more forlorn, he had written to First Assistant Postmaster General J. C. Koons that "I have just returned from a trip to the mills and learned that some time ago (as I was aware) the express office at Port Ludlow was discontinued and closed . . . and that recently an auditor for the Express Company came to the office at Port Gamble, settled up the accounts with the agent at that point, took away their blanks, and said that the office was closed as it did not pay. . . .

"The express companies and the telegraph companies have always, until recently, maintained offices at Port Gamble and Port Ludlow. Today we have no telegraph service and no express service at either place." Those were the same towns that had received baseball scores from San Francisco by telegraph in the 1870s. Now, they were too remote to bother with—too remote, by a kind of circular logic, to connect with the eastern side of the Sound.

The economics of local water transportation had changed in more ways than one, and Ames wasn't the only person distressed by what had happened. In February 1919, Joshua Green of the Puget Sound Navigation Company wrote to Ames that "the [competing] gas boat *Seal* delivered about 35 tons to your store at Port Ludlow a few days ago and it hurt our feelings pretty badly. . . .

"The [Puget Sound Navigation Company's steamboat] *Puget* has lost upwards of $7,000 each year for the past four or five years and . . . we are badly discouraged on the route—it has been mainly . . . your assistance and strong help that has encouraged us to keep a steamer on the run. . . . Unless the poor old *Puget* gets all the revenue there is she is going to be such a loser that we will simply have to give her up." By mutual agreement, a boat that had outlived its usefulness was serving ports that had outlived their usefulness; if either party broke that agreement, Green was saying, economics would run their inevitable course, and both sides would be out of business.

Ames didn't disagree, but he replied a bit testily that "there are times . . . when our freight is of such a nature that your boats do not care to carry it. . . . There have been times in the past when some little boat has been employed to freight to Port Ludlow in particular hay and feed. I understand that your boats refuse to go and pick up feed and hay on the waterways or at other docks without an extra charge of 50 cents per ton. . . . if the extra charge of 50 cents per ton is a proper one . . . it might be to our advantage . . . to absorb [it]."

Green responded with a lesson in post-war economics. "Heretofore," he said, "we have always moved anywhere on the waterfront for 10 tons of freight and [were] glad to do it, but last September when oil went up from 72 cents to $1.87 we found it cost us at least 50 cents per ton in actual fuel to move our boats around the waterfront picking up freight. . . . If we can come into Seattle, tie up to the dock and shut off the oil burners, we can save a great deal of money, but if we have to steam up and move to some outside dock the extra expense is added and as the steamers were not making any money we felt it right to ask the consignee to stand it or haul the freight to Colman Dock. It places us under a handicap as against boats like the *Seal* and other small craft that really have no headquarters in Seattle. . . .

"The farmers at Point Williams have just taken over the dock there and agree to give our company all of their business. Even though *Seal* and other gas boats haul it for less, they feel the regular service will help their district and is worth a little more to them than service via small jobbing gas boats and this is the only argument we can offer you."

The Puget Sound Navigation Company could no longer make what it considered an adequate profit by giving remote communities regular service at a competitive price. If the people who lived in such places wanted regular service, they'd have to pay extra for it. Steamboats no longer qualified as cheap transportation.

Ames knew very well that the economics of water transportation had changed. At the same time he was trying to retain or restore steamboat service to his mill towns, he was trying to break the mills' traditional reliance on water freight. The mills at both Port Gamble and Port Ludlow had been founded for the cargo trade, but under modern conditions, they could no longer rely on it exclusively.

Even from ideal natural harbors, lumber would somehow have to be shipped overland. "We have always up to within this year paid particular attention to the cargo business," Ames wrote to a Boston lumber merchant early in 1919. "Our mills, being situated on the west side of the Sound and 35 miles away from a railroad by water, have not been equipped to do a part of the large business of shipping lumber by rail, which has developed since the railroads came to Puget Sound." He made the coming of the railroads sound like a recent event. They had reached the Sound thirty-six years before.

Pope & Talbot had stuck to the methods of 1853, and time had finally caught up with the firm. "Our trade . . . has been in cargo lots to all foreign ports of the world. . . ," Ames explained, "and also the California trade which we could reach by water. During this past year [though,] we have been making some changes in our plant, particularly at Port Gamble, with the idea of engaging in what we call the rail trade."

The mill began by loading lumber onto rail cars that were resting on moored lighters. Then, it invested in a landing and tracks that enabled the cars to be taken ashore for loading. It was easy enough to barge the cars to the railhead in Seattle, but now Ames—like the halibut fishermen of the late 1880s—had to contend with the fact that instead of being closer to the ocean, the Olympic Peninsula was farther from the railroad. For Ames and a lot of other people, the Sound was coming to seem less a highway than a barrier.

Puget Sound residents welcomed the economic benefits of industrialization (HPCUW, A.C. Warner photo)

In the 1920s, Seattle was the country's main port of entry for Japanese silk (PSMHS/WC, Webster & Stevens)

water pollution had arrived

Until the war, most jobs around Puget Sound were still tied to the cutting of trees and milling of lumber. The lumber industry no longer depended on oxen and single-bitted axes, but it had not progressed far from the nineteenth century, and most of it was still economically marginal. Although the mills cut enormous amounts of lumber, there were so many trees and so many people turning them into boards than even in relatively good times, there was seldom much profit to be had. In bad times, only the big operators could cover their losses, and big operators were few and far between. "There were hundreds of millowners . . . to whom even simple bookkeeping was an esoteric art," Norman Clark has written in *Mill Town*. "Their manufacturing plants were simply a series of rusty saws in leaky shacks, powered by belts from steam engines, locked in a dreary rhythm of overproduction and close-down." Even most of the larger operators had troubles. Clark has written that "after 1900, Jim Hill had brought so many timber men and opened so many forests that the industry was fearfully overexpanded and afflicted with chronic overproduction. When prices dropped, most operators had to cut more wood than before to pay their debts. It was a mad world in which a diminishing demand for their products and a falling price level forced hundreds of millowners to produce twenty-four hours a day until a glutted market refused to take another stick or shingle."

Overproduction remained a problem after the war. It was still possible for a man to put a rusty saw in a leaky shack and call himself a millowner, but the industry, like the region, had started moving farther away from the frontier. There were still mill towns and logging towns, farms without electricity or running water, but in the cities, by the end of the war it was possible to buy electric vacuum cleaners, toasters, waffle irons, washing machines. In 1914, for the first time, the Port of Seattle's domestic imports exceeded its domestic exports. That meant the area was no longer just a colony of California and the industrialized East. It was a market, a processing center, a port of entry. Even after the armistice, there were more domestic imports than exports. While foreign shipping declined, Seattle consolidated its position as the country's main port of entry for Japanese silk, cornering almost the entire silk trade.

New technology and new money found their way into the lumber industry, too. In 1915, Weyerhaeuser, which according to the official corporate history, *Timber and Men*, had never before made a major investment in local processing, had opened a huge, modern mill at Everett, the biggest single sawmill in the world. When the war ended, more capital was put into other large mills. Electrically powered machinery was being installed in factories all over the country; around Puget Sound the larger milling companies took out their old steam engines and brought electric power into their mills. As the 1920s progressed, companies with enough capital also demonstrated that there were alternatives to simply cutting round logs into squared boards. Veneer mills began turning Douglas fir into plywood. And, most importantly of all, the pulp industry arrived.

Pulp mills were nothing new in the United States. Wood pulp had been turned into paper well back in the nineteenth century—but only in older, more easterly parts of the country; never on Puget Sound. The pulp mills brought a real industrial process to the Sound, funneling more capital than ever before into the milling communities, creating more jobs, providing millowners with a level of profit that the chronically depressed lumber industry could not sustain.

In Shelton, the Simpson Timber Company's president, Mark Reed, had established electric lumber and shingle mills. Reed had married into the Simpson family, and, to all intents and purposes, he *was* the company—one of the leading firms in the leading industry in the state. He was also the Republican speaker of the state legislature, perhaps the most powerful single politician in Washington. Unlike the small operators with their rusty saws, Reed had visions of a modern industry. Like the Weyerhaeusers, he had developed timberlands as well as processing plants, assuring himself a long-term supply of raw materials.

He had also lured the Northern Pacific railroad to Shelton, over which he presided as a hard-headed, but in many ways benevolent, industrial despot. By the late 1920s he had helped persuade the Zellerbachs of San Francisco to build the Rainier pulp mill in Shelton. That mill, like both earlier and later mills at Port Angeles, might never have been built without the promotional zeal of a Welsh-born former investment banker named Edward Mills, who became president of the Rainier Pulp and Paper Company. However large a part Mills played, Reed himself had taken an active interest in the building of the Shelton mill. He considered it the vital missing link, the element that would combine with his logging and milling operations to form a complete, rational economic system.

Late in 1929, not yet alarmed by the Wall Street crash but disgusted by the continued irrationality of the lumber industry, Reed wrote that "the lumber business for the last year or two has been going through what seems to me to be the most impossible situation that we have met in a great many years. We have no complaint so far as our logging operation is concerned. . . . With good timber, economically handled, we are able to show a profit, although not as large as we feel we should after . . . two generations. . . .

"The mill end of the game, however, is just simply impossible. We don't seem to have any sense. Lumbermen go out and slash prices, cut each other's throats and raise hell generally, with no seeming objective in view."

Free enterprise still had its drawbacks. There were just too many competitors who could get in with too little capital. The new pulp mills seemed to be saving the day. "Our pulp mill operation is working out splendidly," Reed wrote. "In our mill at Shelton we cut nothing but hemlock lumber which, as you know, without drying is too heavy to ship by rail, so that the entire lumber shipments of the mill go by water. The beauty part of it is that we are utilizing every inch of sound wood that comes into the mill and we are taking at least twenty percent more material off the ground than we were before we had the pulp mill. The waste that we are selling to the pulp mill is helping very materially to bring about an even break of the sawmill operation, even caring for depreciation. Besides selling this waste to the pulp mill we also furnish the fuel to the power plant, which we own, which furnishes the steam and electrical energy for the pulp mill." Fifty years later, that use of waste would be considered unusually progressive. Reed had developed an almost closed system and believed that he had seen the region's economic future. "I feel confident," he said, "that the pulp wood industry is going to be a very important factor in the development of the Northwest in years to come. . . . I am taking some stock in the Port Angeles plant which is now being built and will be probably the largest producer of pulp in the Northwest."

If the pulp industry brought the promise of economic stability and the reality of jobs and income, it also brought new sights and smells to the communities around Puget Sound. Industrial processes weren't entirely new to the Sound. The Tacoma smelter, operating since 1889, had long since burdened the downwind soil with deposits of lead and other heavy metals that seem likely to endure forever. Smoke from the burning of sawdust and slash often filled the air, and thick blankets of smoke from forest fires had been endemic since the time of the earliest white settlers. Still, the hanging sulfurous stench of the pulp mills, the stench that would enable even small children to recognize mill towns with their eyes closed, was something quite new. Equally new was the sight of pulp liquor flowing in distinct streams out into the waters of the Sound.

Water pollution had arrived. People had always dumped things into the Sound, of course. But there was a difference between the waste from a cannery, on which crabs and various fish could grow fat, and the pulp liquor, in which not even barnacles could grow. Anacortes, for example, had long had a cannery that, like all canneries, dropped its waste directly into the water, sometimes creating such a stench that the citizens rose in revolt. The town also had a point, known as Snider's Point, where it was convenient for nearby citizens to back their wagons up to a low bank and toss their garbage over the edge, onto the mudflats below. The tide would come in and cover the garbage. The tide would go out and the garbage would be gone. The method was crude, but it didn't harm marine life in the bay. Kids with nothing else to do could go down to the beach, start a driftwood fire, set out crab pots made by stretching wire over wheel rims or old tires, haul in heavy loads of huge crabs, and while away the day by cooking their catch in old oil cans filled with sea water. As soon as the pulp mill started disgorging pulp liquor into Padilla Bay, the kids stopped catching crabs. The crabs didn't seem to be there any more.

That was really no surprise. It had already been observed elsewhere in the country that aquatic life did not benefit from the presence of sulfite pulp mills. Still, not many people around Puget Sound had been concerned; the concern had been concentrated among the people who stood to lose the most in the shortest time, the commercial oystermen.

Oysters had been harvested commercially in sheltered waters at the southern end of the Sound for decades. By the 1920s, the oyster beds were protected by networks of dikes. The harvesting and sale of oysters did not constitute a major industry on the level of salmon fishing and processing, but it was a significant business of some standing, and the oystermen had a lively sense of their own self-interest.

In June 1926, the Olympia Oyster Growers' Association wrote to State Supervisor of Fisheries Charles R. Pollock about "the installation of a paper mill at Shelton, Washington, and the proposed installation of other paper mills and manufacturing plants on the head waters of Puget Sound. . . .

"The trade waste coming from such proposed manufacturing plants, if permitted to go into tide waters or the streams flowing therein will destroy or be highly deleterious to fish, clams, oysters and other sea life. The proposed plant at Shelton, which is only a few miles from the most valuable oyster preserves the state has, would, if permitted to run the trade waters into Oakland Bay, entirely destroy the state's preserves and, as well, all privately owned oyster beds in that vicinity, if we are clearly informed. . . .

"The Oyster Growers' Association desires to appeal to your office for protection."

The Shelton plant seemed particularly ominous because of its location, but it was clearly just one of many plants that would soon be built on Puget Sound. The locations of all the new plants would be somewhat ominous to the oyster growers. Inevitably, the plants would be built in the old coastal mill towns that had grown up beside enclosed, sheltered bays that offered safe anchorage for sailing ships. Those enclosed waters would trap the effluents from the mills. If pollutants escaped from the mill town harbors, they might be trapped farther along the coast in the bays in which oysters were grown. No one knew how many mills would ultimately be built. When the oyster growers held their annual meeting in July, a State Department of Health sanitary engineer named H. W. Nightingale told them, "The foundation for a plant said to be 100 ton daily capacity is being installed at Shelton. A company is planning a similar plant at Boston Harbor and another company is said to be contemplating the installation of a pulp mill on Chuckanut Bay.

"The construction engineer at Shelton could give us no information about plans for disposal of the water sulphite liquor at that plant. . . . "At Anacortes I observed the dumping of red pulp liquor into the sea water adjoining the mill. It is reported that shipworms on the adjoining wharf have been killed since the waste has been going into the water. Crabs have also left the vicinity, according to a similar report. . . .

"The red pulp liquor and white water are unquestionably deleterious to fish and shell-fish life."

The next month, the State Health Department suggested that "if any more pulp and paper plants are allowed to be built in the State of Washington without due regard to the proper care of the waste . . . the entire natural resource vested in the marine life of the state will be greatly impaired and possibly destroyed."

At the end of August, the chairman of the Washington State Fisheries Board appointed an Investigation Committee on Pollution Problems.

At the beginning of September, the executive committee of the Association of Pacific Fisheries said that "the unrestricted operation of paper and pulp mills on Puget Sound . . . can only result in serious pollution . . . with consequent loss of valuable parts of the salmon fisheries. . . . The least these plants can do is to so treat their wastes that they will not become a menace to the salmon and oyster industries."

When the Investigation Committee on Pollution Problems met the following January, the report of the meeting said, "The following note was received yesterday from C. C. Hunt, a fish dealer in Anacortes:

Top: Paper making, c. 1927 (TPL, Boland photo)

*Bottom: Oyster beds flourished behind dike enclosures in
southern Puget Sound (HPCUW, Asahel Curtis photo)*

Dear Sir:

I am very much afraid that the poison chemicals from the pulp mills are destroying the crabs . . . etc. around here and also in all of the Puget Sound territory. I think there should be an investigation before it is too late.

"Only this morning one of the Fisheries Inspectors handed the Supervisor a report that in the bay at Port Angeles, boatmen claim they keep the hulls of their boats clean if they can be moored opposite the pulp mill which discharges its waste water into the head of the bay. Likewise, shingle mill men advised him that they moor their bolts [of cedar] in that end of the bay if possible to keep the bolts free of marine growth."

The report observed that "this state . . . is now almost free from intense pollution" but left little doubt that the situation was about to change. People were "clamoring for new industries," it said, and they weren't even considering the value of the old industries that would be destroyed. Traditionally, all the many uses of the water had been able to coexist. Now, the Sound was going to be fought over by industries that were basically incompatible. The conflict was inescapable, and its immediate outcome was never in doubt.

The mill at Shelton started up with no time—and, presumably, no sleep—lost for consideration of the oyster beds or oystermen. Almost immediately, the oysters in southern Puget Sound took a turn for the worse. The oyster spawn did not survive. The yield of the beds declined. The oystermen saw their living and their way of life going down the drain.

In July 1929, Martha Deer, the wife of oysterman Joe Deer, wrote to Mark Reed that "I would not lay a straw in the way of (the) Progress and Prosperity of Shelton . . . [but] Mr. Reed, the only source of our mantance (sic) is being distroyed (sic) and we are going to be left stranded. . . . We had taken care of the oyster beds, improved them, repaired dykes and added to our necesary (sic) equipment and took care of the obligation we owed you. . . . we have put back [into] the oyster beds every thing we had to spare. Our house needs a roof and paint badly . . . which we had planned to do but now we can't." (Oysterman E. N. Steele, in his *Rise and Decline of the Olympia Oyster Industry*, recalled that Joe Deer and various other oystermen in the Oakland Bay "were all progressive men. . . . In the earlier days Oakland Bay was the most prolific oyster seed ground in the world. Transportation from there to the packing plants in Olympia was very difficult. Not long after the commercial value of the Olympia oysters was discovered, J. H. Deer built and operated an opening and packing plant in Shelton which met the need of the oyster growers in that locality.")

Reed was being put on the spot, but it was a spot that left him plenty of room to maneuver. He was viewed as the main spokesman and apologist for the pulp mill, which he had brought to Shelton, but he did not own much stock in, and did not manage, the mill. He owned oyster beds himself, and he had demonstrated a concern for the welfare of the town he and his business interests dominated. He played his roles off against each other and took a position of judicious detachment: yes, something was wrong, but there was no proof that the pulp mill was responsible—a contention that was technically correct—and in the absence of proof, hasty action was uncalled for.

"You have my sincere sympathy," he wrote to Mrs. Deer. "I am just as much at sea as you are. I am frank to say it has not been demonstrated to me (that is, satisfactorily) that the pulp mill is responsible for the lack of a seed catch on the oyster beds for the last few years. My interest in the pulp mill is very nominal and does not compare in amount to my investment in the oyster beds. . . . this would appear to be a favorable year for oyster propagation and the next few months should demonstrate to a great extent the cause of your trouble.

From the oystermen's point of view, the next few months showed more clearly than ever that the pulp mill was to blame. Reed still wasn't convinced.

"There is something fundamentally wrong with conditions, we must all agree," he wrote on October 14, but "no one seems to know what it is at this time."

Reed's political coyness notwithstanding, the facts of the situation have never been totally beyond dispute. The number of oysters harvested behind dikes had never approached the number harvested from wild beds early in the century. As the wild populations were depleted, though, dike culture became the industry's only hope for survival. The dikes did not protect oysters from climatic conditions, silt deposits or predators. The mill companies attributed the declining oyster populations to those natural causes and the imprudence of individual oystermen. The oystermen, in turn, were sure that pollution from the mills was decisive.

"Personally," Reed wrote, "I am not sponsoring the pulp mill's position nor the oyster men's position, but I do want to see that a fairly conducted investigation of the problem is had, . . . Oakland Bay is not the only bay that has suffered materially for the past three years and Oakland Bay is not the only bay that has been denuded of its oyster supply. I believe the state and government officials are approaching this investigation with a fair and determined mind. . . . We cannot afford to have our oyster industry crippled or destroyed and let us hope that it will not be."

Presumably Reed sincerely did hope that it would not be, but hope was not enough. Conditions kept getting worse. The issue did not go away. The oystermen kept pushing, and Reed continued to be viewed—and to conduct himself—as the spokesman for industrialization. On December 23, 1930, he wrote, "We had a rather large, interested and sympathetic meeting last evening of citizens of Shelton, where an opportunity was given to express both sides of the controversy between the pulp mill and the oystermen. The community is thoroughly aroused; in fact, so much so that there is little or nothing else being talked of. A general committee of twenty-five was appointed, who in turn is to appoint a smaller committee to see what can be done to work out the problem, and there seems to be an earnest desire to do . . . whatever is necessary to save the industrial program of the city."

There was no doubt in Reed's mind that the pulp mill was the key to that "industrial program," and that it had to be kept running. Evidently, he viewed the mill as a higher stage of economic evolution—which in a sense it was—and at least some people at the meeting found his arguments persuasive. The next day, the Reverend F. E. Dark wrote to Reed about his "very clear and convincing statement regarding the pulp mill situation.

"I have never questioned the value of the mill to our town nor the desirability of retaining it here," Dark said. "It has been difficult however, for me to get away from the thought the oystermen had priority . . . here and that an injustice was being done them. In my own thinking I have offset this with the argument that in industrial matters justice consists in the greatest good to the largest number and from this standpoint justice is on the side of the pulp mill.

"Your statement last night put the whole matter in a different light. . . .

"I was . . . much interested in the clearcut way in which (you) presented the industrial development here culminating in the coming of the pulp plant."

Reed's position in the community was patriarchal, and it is hard to separate useful rhetoric from a genuine feeling of responsibility. "I think I can honestly say," he wrote to Dark, "that my original thought in bringing the pulp mill to Shelton was to be helpful to the community; and the great interest I have now is only that of protecting our citizenship who have made such material investments, some of them their all, in purchasing homes and enlarging their business activities. . . . I have hopes that some plan can be worked out which will save this very important industry to our little city."

Just over a year ago he had written that "the waste . . . we are selling to the pulp mill is helping very materially to bring about an even break of the sawmill operation, even caring for depreciation," and discussed his own growing investment in the pulp industry.

Right: Mark Reed

Middle: Oyster shucking (HPCUW)

Bottom: Simpson Logging Company crew,
c. 1929 (HPCUW, Clark Kinsey photo)

Still, it was not totally unrealistic to link the pulp mill with the general welfare. Even in the best of times the jobs and income provided by a pulp mill would have been extremely important to Shelton or almost any other town around the Sound.

By the fall of 1930, the times were dreadful. The depression was a year old. Jobs were scarce. The lumber industry, which had trouble even during the economic boom of the 1920s, was in dreadful shape. Reed and other mill owners who were concerned about the welfare of their work forces, the long-term future of their industry, or both, tried desperately just to keep the mills running. The fight for a tariff to protect Northwestern lumber from Canadian competition had failed; the powerful eastern congressmen had less of a stake in Northwestern prosperity than they had in cheap lumber.

By May, Reed was writing, "About two weeks ago I reduced the price of logs about $1.20 per thousand, and yesterday five of my customers waited on me and asked for a further reduction of one dollar or they were fearful they would have to close down. It may be, in order to keep them running, that we will have to. . . . There just does not seem to be any bottom to the market, and I feel that we cannot allow our customers to close down, throwing the men out of employment, and allow the self-log-supplying mills to continue to operate. . . . beginning the first of June, 80 per cent of the operators have agreed to a curtailment program whereby two-shift mills go to one shift, and one-shift mills go to five days per week. . . . Weyerhaeuser and Long-Bell have agreed to take off shifts. This will probably reduce the production of lumber about 25 per cent, which still is not enough. . . . The market is absorbing somewhere from 40 to 50 per cent. . . . All we have to do, I presume, is keep a stiff upper lip and keep the wheels turning, if we can."

Even under different circumstances, of course, Reed would hardly have been eager to see the pulp mill close, and whatever the state of the economy, he was an extremely powerful man.

With powerful opposition *and* the depression to contend with, the oystermen didn't stand a chance. They kept fighting and protesting anyway. A number of oystermen in the Shelton area sued the pulp mill and received payments out of court. After a while, the more politically conscious companies had their mills try to release the most visible pollutants at night. But night or day, the mills kept operating and the industry grew, just as Reed had predicted it would. In towns around the Sound, the plants represented the largest concentrations of capital and jobs. Economically and politically, oysters weren't in the same league.

*The National Guard was called in during the 1935 Tacoma
strike (HSSKC/P.I., Art French photo)*

give this great natural resource back to the people

Business had been romanticized during the 1920s, when the first pulp mills were built, but in the depression years that followed, the romanticism disappeared. Throughout the country, the 1930s were characterized by suspicion and hostility toward business, by massive labor-organizing drives, and bitter strikes. The Sound was no longer the national center of labor radicalism—the general strike of the 1930s took place in San Francisco—but business was on the defensive there, too. In Seattle, a 1934 dock strike, part of a larger West Coast dock strike, saw pickets effectively barricade the piers. Strike-breakers were taken by launch to the seaward side of Pier 40, where they set up quarters in a moored freighter. Mounted police finally got a train onto Pier 40 by clearing the way with a cavalry charge at 4:00 A.M. In 1935, there was a long, bitter strike of mill workers, which finally forced Weyerhaeuser, among others, to formally recognize a union, and which gave rise to a steady stream of violent conflicts between strikers and strikebreakers, and confrontations between strikers and police. In Tacoma, city officials were pleading for a proclamation of martial law. Clubs and gas were used on strikers there, some of the gas being sprayed from the exhausts of National Guard trucks. One newspaper photographer caught a shirtsleeved crowd in a Tacoma street being driven back by a line of national guardsmen with fixed bayonets. At the same time, waterfront unions were calling a twenty-four-hour strike as a memorial to strikers killed the year before.

Organized labor wasn't the only segment of society that had grown disenchanted. The federal government wasn't as probusiness under Roosevelt as it had been under Harding, Coolidge, and Hoover. Not only was it regulating business more closely; it was also stepping into areas that had previously been left to private enterprise. One was the generation of electric power. In the Southeast, the government set up the Tennessee Valley Authority. In the Northwest, it began building huge power and irrigation dams along the Columbia River. Publicly owned dams on the Columbia would use the public's water to generate publicly owned power.

Public ownership of public resources was a popular idea. The concentration of public resources in corporate hands was not. On Puget

Sound, a disproportionate number of salmon and steelhead—which everyone considered a public resource—had been funneled into the fish trap owners' hands for generations. The time was ripe for a political campaign against the traps. Both commercial and sport fishermen took advantage of it.

Almost no one who caught salmon or steelhead trout with nets or with rod and reel had ever liked the traps. Fish traps were just too efficient, took too many of the fish and left too few for anyone else. As competition for the fish grew more intense, the traps became less popular than ever.

The nature of the competition had changed dramatically. By the end of World War I, the commercial fishing fleet in Puget Sound bore little resemblance to the collection of rowboats that had chased salmon at the turn of the century. Gasoline motors had become widespread by the beginning of the war, increasing the efficiency and range of net-fishing boats, and allowing the establishment of a coastal trolling fleet—mainly Norwegian immigrants and their families—that used the Sound as home base. The first marine diesel engine—more reliable and much safer than the early gas engines—appeared around 1914. After the war, diesels proliferated. They were crude—one retired fisherman recalls an early Swedish model so large and noisy that each piston stroke sounded like an explosion—but they worked. The 1929 diesel put into Phil Green's purse seiner *Janet G.*, the last boat of any consequence built at a commercial yard on Vashon, weighed ten and one-half tons. The fly wheel alone weighed a ton and a half. The engine was bulky, but it was reliable and then some; it worked even better at the end of World War II than it did when the boat was launched.

With better motors and bigger boats, the fishermen were ranging farther afield. At the end of World War I, seiners from Puget Sound began cruising north to Alaska. Fuel was cheap—in the 1920s, a trip from Seattle to Ketchikan could be made for $8.45—and there were plenty of fish. The annual northward migration became—as it still is—a part of many Puget Sound fishermen's way of life.

On the Sound itself, the bigger boats with more powerful engines were going after fewer and fewer fish. Partly because of the Fraser River rockslide, partly because of water pollution, and partly because of overfishing, the salmon catch in Puget Sound plummeted. The salmon catch during the five years of World War I was only about sixteen percent larger than the catch in the single record year of 1913. Nevertheless, it was greater than the catch during the entire decade of the 1920s.

The traps, concentrated chiefly in the northern Sound, took the lion's share of this shrinking resource. During the period from 1921 to 1930, there was an average of 1,174 commercial boats licensed on the Sound each year. In 1930, there were licenses for just 257 traps—not all the licenses were used; fish companies bought extra licenses to keep competitors from using certain spots—and 172 of them were controlled by just nine operators. During the years from 1921 through 1930, the traps took fifty-eight percent of the sockeye salmon caught in Puget Sound, fifty-one percent of the silvers, forty percent of the humpbacked or pink salmon, and eighty-two percent of the kings. No wonder the commercial fishermen were resentful.

Phil Green's son Joe has recalled that his father was offered consulting jobs deciding where to put fish traps in southeast Alaska. He could have made a lot of money at a time when money was hard to come by, but he refused. He always refused to have anything to do with the traps.

By themselves, the commercial fishermen might not have been any more effective than the oystermen. But after a while, they weren't alone in their opposition to traps.

Since the earliest days of white settlement, people had caught salmon and steelhead for sport, as well as for food and money. Clarence Bagley, in his *History of King County, Washington*, had, in fact, talked somewhat disparagingly of the nineteenth-century Indian's doggedly practical reluctance to catch salmon for sport.

In many ways, then as now, the most attractive fish to sport fishermen was not the salmon but the steelhead trout. Unlike the salmon, the steelhead is still feeding when it enters the rivers, and can be caught with rods and flies. By the end of World War I, steelhead fishermen formed a small but dedicated group—just the sort of group one would expect to be formed by people whose chosen pastime requires standing hip-deep in moving water in the dead of winter.

The steelheaders had several concerns: poachers were using gillnets inside the river mouths to capture steelhead swimming toward the spawning beds; although there were state fish-and-game laws, the laws were enforced by county governments, which did a ludicrously ineffective job; last but not least, steelhead were being caught in fish traps.

Some of the hardest core steelheaders belonged to the Seattle Sportsmen's Association, but they were frustrated there. They formed a small minority of the membership, and their concerns got little attention. In 1928, they broke away and founded the Steelhead Trout Club of Washington.

The club promptly launched a campaign against the poachers. It wanted the state to ban all winter net fishing inside river mouths. As allies, the steelheaders enlisted the purse seiners who were skeptical at first, but who joined in after they learned that the poachers were taking pink and silver salmon, too. (Presumably, the seiners weren't entirely reluctant to take a swipe at even legitimate gillnetters—in 1924, gillnetters had tried to pass an initiative that would have banned purse seines,

Above: in the summer of 1934, backers of Initiative 77 delivered 80,000 signatures to the State capitol. Right: Ken McLeod.

as well as traps.) In 1929, the state legislature declared steelhead a game fish in fresh water above the mouths of most rivers; it was still a legitimate target for net fishermen out on salt water, but inside the rivers, it was protected.

Three years later, the steelheaders provided leadership for a successful campaign to put on the statewide ballot Initiative 62, which established statewide departments of fish and game. In its original form, the initiative included a paragraph that would have permitted the new state game department to designate game fish. Underlying that paragraph was an assumption that the department would make the steelhead a game fish exclusively, so that it could no longer be caught with nets or in traps even in the salt water of the Sound.

The steelhead had never been very important commercially: it had never been plentiful enough. But during the winter months, when other fish weren't running, trap owners did derive some income from the steelhead, which were iced and loaded on fast trains for the luxury markets of New York and France.

Although the luxury trade in steelhead didn't bring in much money, the big canning companies that operated the fish traps saw no reason to give up what little profit there was. The canners had a lot of money and a lot of political power. In the state legislature, where their interests were guarded by Mark Reed's political crony E. A. Sims, they had the power to kill any bill that they felt threatened canning interests. During the Initiative 62 campaign, the trade group that represented the canners served notice that unless the offending paragraph was removed, the canners' money and power would be used against the initiative. The paragraph came out.

The initiative passed narrowly. It was unpopular in eastern Washington, but it got enough votes in counties around Puget Sound to become state law. With the offending paragraph removed, it didn't touch the fish traps.

Both steelheaders and commercial fishermen were still eager to get rid of the traps. Ken McLeod, a former Seattle newspaper columnist who was active in all the steelheaders' lobbying and initiative drives of that period, remembers that steelheaders from Olympia started the campaign for an initiative to abolish the traps. Other steelheaders who had been active in the Initiative 62 fight felt that the time wasn't ripe, McLeod says, but they went along. The commercial fishermen went along, too. Both commercial and sport fishermen supported the Salmon Conservation League, the group formed to pass Initiative 77 and abolish the traps. McLeod and Phil Green were both on the executive committee. The initiative's backers delivered 80,000 signatures to Olympia in June 1934, and the measure was put on the ballot for November.

Fish traps were once legal on Puget Sound. From traps, fish were brailed into scows for delivery to canneries. On the day the bottom photograph was taken, 40,000 salmon were caught in this trap operated by Pacific American Fisheries of Bellingham.

Some commercial fishermen felt later—some still feel—that although they put up most of the money for the campaign, the sportsmen got all the credit. They were basically right. The commercial fishermen did provide most of the funds for the Initiative 77 campaign, with the purse seiners contributing by far the biggest chunk. The sportsmen's manpower and public relations skills were crucial, though.

The campaign for Initiative 77 was basically ambiguous, combining but never fully reconciling appeals to conservation and to populism. In the midst of the depression, after a disastrous commercial fishing season, the initiative was also billed as an economic recovery measure. If passed, it would "be the absolute saving of Washington's third-largest industry," the main pro-77 brochure claimed. It would "create new employment." There would be more "purse seine boats . . . in the open waters, employing eight men to the boat, whereas each trap employes an average of but two men." The number of trollers would increase, too.

The brochure made the connection—one which was rarely appreciated at the time—between recreation and cold, hard cash. Abolition of fish traps, by making the Sound "a sport fisherman's paradise," would bring "hundreds of thousands of dollars to many diversified lines of trade from tourists who now do their salmon fishing in Canada and Alaska because Puget Sound is fished out." It would also "enhance property values through the entire 2,000 miles of shoreline on Puget Sound."

The brochure also talked about what a menace the traps were to immature salmon, which "become fouled in the heavily tarred, grass-choked meshes or are run into pots." The appeal to conservation was sincere, but it was basically nonsense. Properly regulated traps probably posed less of a threat to the fish than a horde of small boats equipped with nets. People disliked the traps not because they were destructive but because they were efficient. They were "wasteful" primarily in that they made it impossible to divide a public resource among a broad spectrum of the public. They were, in fact, monopolized by a handful of big capitalists.

Basically, the brochure argued, these capitalists were getting rich at public expense. "Trap sites are obtained for a fee of only $50 per year to the state and can be held perpetually," it said, although "some of the choice fish trap locations have been sold for as high as $100,000 among big operators." It was a good time to be attacking the "big operator," especially the big operator who pulled financial strings from a distance. The brochure's crucial argument was that the passage of Initiative 77 would "give this great natural resource back to the people instead of leaving it in the hands of a powerful financial minority involving large interests of Eastern and California capital."

The trap interests countered this argument by suggesting that at least the traps put the salmon into the hands of real Americans. Many of the seiners were Slavic immigrants, and some were immigrants from Norway and other European nations. Consequently, the anti-77 forces argued that the initiative was "not a conservation measure"—which was true—"but is the effort of the purse seiners to wrest from the pioneers of Washington their means of livelihood." The anti-77 forces also argued, quite accurately, that abolition of the traps would simply leave more of the Fraser River sockeye for the Canadians.

Evidently, the campaign against 77 went well beyond the bounds of rhetoric. McLeod remembers being in Seattle with Dr. L. W. Whitlow, the president of the Salmon Conservation League, when E. A. Sims, who was running the campaign against 77, invited Whitlow to the Washington Athletic Club to talk. McLeod went along. He remembers that Sims, accompanied by fish packers and trap owners from Bellingham and Seattle, urged both him and Whitlow to abandon the initiative campaign. Finally, late at night, he and Whitlow left. A Seattle fish packer followed them out to the street. On the sidewalk, he told Whitlow and McLeod that if they abandoned the initiative, they'd receive five thousand dollars apiece.

The Seattle packer's offer of cash dovetailed beautifully with the major theme of the 77 campaign: the ability of concentrated capital to monopolize what should be, and by rights was, a public resource. The last issue of the *Vashon Island News Record* before the November election carried a long letter from "Thoralf Jorgensen, Boat Owner and Fisherman," which said, "The fishermen on Vashon and Maury Islands hope that on November 6 all the voters will join them and vote 'FOR' Initiative Measure No. 77, the Salmon Conservation Bill. . . .

"Initiative No. 77 is a fight between thousands of . . . citizens of this state [and] a mere handful of wealthy fish barons. . . .

"[It] will provide profitable employment to a minimum of 30,000 citizens of this state with the runs of salmon built back to the 1913 level. It will permit these 30,000 citizens to share equally in their rightful ownership of the great salmon runs, because these salmon runs belong to all the people, and not to a small group of wealthy fish trap owners and eastern capitalists."

Those arguments had a lot of popular appeal. The initiative passed handily, with seventy percent of the vote.

With the traps gone, there was no serious opposition to making steelhead a game fish, and the legislature made it one the next year.

Also, as the opponents of Initiative 77 had predicted, with the traps gone, the bulk of the Fraser River sockeye run was caught by Canadians. By then, the Canadians had been harvesting the smaller part of the Fraser River run for two generations. Since before World War I, they had been working for a treaty that would both save the fish and divide the catch equally between Canada and the United States. The big Puget Sound canning companies had never agreed. They wanted either no treaty or a treaty that would leave their share of the fish intact at the expense of the smaller companies and the purse seiners. At least twice, their attorneys had helped draw up such treaties, but opposition from the smaller canners and the seiners had kept the treaties from being signed. One was rejected by the Washington State legislature despite a high-pressure lobbying effort in 1919. Another had been approved by American negotiators in 1929 and 1930 but never ratified. This second treaty was still hanging in a diplomatic limbo when the voters of Washington passed Initiative 77.

By abolishing the fish traps that had taken most of the Fraser River catch, the initiative changed the whole situation. In 1935, the first year since at least the 1880s when there had been no American traps in Puget Sound, the American share of the Fraser River catch plummeted to thirteen percent. Suddenly, there was an incentive to sign a treaty that would guarantee the United States half the fish. There was also no longer a need to accommodate the interests of the big trap owners.

After the fishing season of 1935, Washington's senators, Schwellenbach and Bone, asked Dr. Whitlow, now the former chairman of the Salmon Conservation League, to form and chair a committee that could make a Fraser River treaty acceptable. Whitlow recruited five other veterans of the initiative campaign, including McLeod and Green. They worked out the difficulties first with American fishermen, then with the Canadians, and finished their jobs in May 1936. The Senate ratified the treaty in June, Canada ratified it a year later, and it went into effect in August 1937. The United States and Canada were to split evenly the fish that reached the river by swimming through the Strait of Juan de Fuca and the upper Sound. (Salmon that swam south through Johnstone Strait were to remain exclusively Canadian.) The fishery was to be managed jointly by the two nations through an International Pacific Salmon Fisheries Commission. Beginning in 1944, fish ladders were to be built around the Hells Gate rockslide.

The ladders were built, joint management worked, and the Fraser River salmon runs not only survived, they recovered somewhat. But they never recovered totally. The lingering impact of the rockslide was probably not the only reason; the environment in many crucial places had grown less hospitable to fish, and the number of fishermen had increased.

Despite the undoubtedly sincere rhetoric of Initiative 77's supporters, the abolition of fish traps did not create a golden age for the Puget Sound salmon fishery. The region's economic future could be seen clearly in 1935—it was not out on the water, where men in wooden

The Boeing B-17 was touted as the largest airplane in the
United States and the fastest bomber in the world (Boeing photos)

boats now had only each other to fight over salmon runs that the pioneers would have thought pathetic. The future was outside a hangar at Boeing Field, south of Seattle, where fifty men were pushing out a brand-new, four-engine bomber with a wing span of 105 feet. The new plane was the "largest airplane in the United States and reputedly the fastest bomber in the world," reported the *Post-Intelligencer*. It had been built in "utmost secrecy," but it could be hidden no longer. War was approaching in both Europe and the Pacific, and planes made by Boeing, which had been building aircraft in Seattle since 1916—originally building them of wood—were going to play a major part in it. The war, not the abolition of fish traps, was going to revive the depressed economy of Puget Sound.

If the fish trap fight did not produce a millenium, it did at least popularize the idea that the resources of Puget Sound belonged to everyone. Initiative 77 was an assertion that fishery resources were public and shouldn't be concentrated in a few wealthy hands. It was also a declaration that the use of those resources should be determined by criteria that weren't primarily economic. Whatever the profit that lay in supplying sport fishermen, making steelhead a game fish was a triumph of recreational values over economic ones. Leaving the commercial fishery entirely in the hands of the boat fishermen was also an assertion of non-economic values. Economically, a fish trap was far and away the most efficient way to catch salmon. When integrated into the canning industry, the traps were the fishing tool that could generate the greatest profits. By passing Initiative 77, the voters rejected economic efficiency to gain the social benefit of spreading the wealth around and of allowing the largest possible number of small-boat fishermen to survive as independent businessmen. The steelheaders and commercial fishermen were parts of a distinct local culture, a collective regional self-image, and when the voters had to choose, they chose that culture and that self-image over economic rationality.

Most Puget Sound communities emerged from World War II still oriented toward the water. Many were still oriented toward the falling and sawing of timber. Top: Tacoma waterfront in the late 1920s (TPL, Boland photo). Bottom: Bellingham, c. 1945 (WMHA).

the magnificent body of water was now in the way

Around Puget Sound, as elsewhere, the 1920s and 1930s were a transitional period, a time of intense, but unfinished social and economic change that followed the major turning point of World War I. It took the great upheaval of World War II to complete the transition. If the first world war basically ended the economic and social structure of the nineteenth century, the second catapulted everything and everyone into the middle of the twentieth.

The Puget Sound economy was less primitive at the start of the second world war than it had been at the start of the first, but the wartime transformation was similar. Again, the shipyards boomed. The modern ferry *Kalakala* was employed chiefly to carry workers from Seattle to the naval shipyard at Bremerton. New yards sprang up. In 1939, the shipbuilding industry had been valued at only $6.5 million. By 1943, the Bremerton yard and sixteen private yards around Puget Sound had contracts for two hundred ships worth $700 million. That was more than the total value of all manufacturing in the state of Washington in 1939. The Boeing aircraft factories in Seattle and Renton also mushroomed during the war, Boeing's work force expanding in four years from 4,000 to 45,000. The canneries were busy, lumber was selling, and the ports, particularly Seattle, were important shipping points for the Pacific theater. Workers moved in from all over the country to take jobs in the defense industries. New housing was thrown up to accommodate them. The whole state was gaining population, and more and more of the new people were concentrating around Puget Sound. In Kitsap County, site of the navy yard, the population by mid-1942 had increased ninety percent.

The second wartime boom didn't last any longer than the first had. Still, the regional economy had changed irrevocably by 1945, and the Sound communities that emerged from the war weren't quite the same ones that had entered it. Most were still oriented toward the water. Many were still oriented toward the falling and sawing of timber. The 1950 revision of the original 1941 WPA writers' guide to Washington described most of the cities around the Sound in terms that might have been appropriate ten, twenty, or fifty years back. In Bellingham, it said, "industrial life is concentrated along the water front, where squarely massed warehouses, coal bunkers and piers are punctuated with the black smokestacks of mills and factories, harsh against the green hills. Moored at the docks are large, ocean-going freighters, sturdy cannery tenders, numerous small fishing boats and trim pleasure craft. From the bayside, streets radiate into the business and residential areas."

In Everett, too, "the industrial life of the city centers in the area along the bayside and the river front. Here, fringing the city, are factories and mills with their stacks and burners, smoking volcanoes by day and glowing infernos by night. Except when a holiday or curtailed production brings a temporary lull, the air reverberates with the whine of saws, the strident blasts of whistles, the hiss of steam and the clack of wheels as engines shunt cars of freight on the sidings.

"Moored along the docks are freighters, their strong booms swinging incoming cargo to the docks and outgoing cargo, mostly lumber and lumber products, to the decks and into the holds. . . . Dotting the bay are numerous pleasure craft, trawlers, sturdy tugs with rafts of logs in tow, and rowboats. . . .

"The salt air is charged with the pungent odor of seaweed from the brine-soaked tidelands, the resinous tang of newly cut lumber and of smoke from the burning slabs and sawdust, the clean odor of tar from nets and creosoted pilings, and the musty smell of rotting logs, heavy with barnacles. At night, the low, musical throb of Diesel engines and the impatient chugging of gasoline motors float across the water, or the whistle of a train, clear and resonant, echoes through the moisture-laden air.

"Here is registered the heartbeat of Everett."

In Olympia, which, of course, had the burgeoning industry of state government just up the hill from the harbor, "sawmills and woodworking plants, knitting mills and oyster-packing houses cover the area between the east and west bays. . . . Adjacent to the mitten-shaped tideflat is anchorage deep enough for ocean-going freighters; and in the shallow waters nearby are the beds of the delicious Olympia oyster."

Even Tacoma, which by the war's end had slightly less than one-third the population of Seattle, rated a similar description. There, "along the bay and on the flats are sawmills, factories for lumber products, railroad shops and other industrial establishments, including two important electro-chemical plants. Railroad tracks are lined with freight cars and switch engines. The penetrating smell of tideland mingles with the resinous fragrance from piles of newly cut lumber. Sometimes the air is heavy with the pungent smell of sulphur from the pulp mills. To the northwest is the towering smokestack of the Tacoma smelter, one of the two highest stacks in the world and visible for miles, with its drifting trail of light, lemon-colored smoke. . . . Steamships from all parts of the world are busily loading and unloading cargo; puffing tugs with tows of logs, slow freighters and small craft and fishing smacks dot the bay. Gulls wheel on flashing white wings or perch on floating logs, old pilings or dock roofs, on the alert for refuse dumped from the galleys of passing steamers. Always the tang of salt water is in the air, redolent of seaweed on hot summer days or sharp and fresh when a brisk wind sweeps inland from Puget Sound."

Seattle was a bit different. There was plenty of waterfront activity to write about, but this was clearly not a mill town, or even a mill town at one remove. "From Smith Cove at the left, north of the metropolitan area, to Alki Point at the right, runs a saw-toothed rim of piers, docks and wharves broken only on the south by tide flats and the Duwamish River, which forks around the man-made Harbor Island. Beyond the water front and Alaskan Way, a broad commercial avenue, are the warehouses and the factories, and behind them the ragged skyline of the business area. . . .

"Locomotives noisily shunt their cars, and trucks rumble along the wide, dock-lined street. Stevedores expertly load and unload slings swung by booms and squeaking winches. Tug boats whistle petulantly and ferries push their way in and out of the slips. . . . From unostentatious docks and from piers longer than any in the country, vessels depart for Alaska and the Orient. And the seagulls drift out over the entire city, coming to rest everywhere."

The regional economic changes brought by the war weren't always visible in individual cities and towns. In many communities the sawmill or pulp mill or cannery was still the most important industry. For the region as a whole, though, Boeing dwarfed the canneries and mills. Shipyard employment had declined sharply when the war ended, although the Bremerton navy yard remained the largest single employer on the Kitsap Peninsula and continued to draw workers from the east side of the Sound. White-collar employment grew in Seattle and the other cities. Aluminum refining, drawn to Tacoma and other points in Washington during the war by the cheap electricity generated at Columbia River dams, provided another alternative to fish and forest products.

Around the densely populated fringes of the Sound, the forests weren't quite what they had been. Lumber production in the twelve counties around Puget Sound had been 5.79 million board feet in 1926, only 2.96 million in 1940. By 1950, it was down to 2.05 million, only two-thirds the 1926 figure for King, Pierce, Kitsap, and Thurston counties alone.

"The forests, the fisheries and the soils of the region already give indication that the cream-skimming stage is past," noted a 1948 article in the Harvard Business Review. The proliferation of tractors and trucks had created a place in the woods for small "gypo" logging outfits of five or ten or twenty men. At the other end of the economic scale, the decline of the forests and the increase of operating costs had forced the larger companies to become integrated, processing-oriented industries, using more of what had formerly been left on the forest floor or disposed of at the mill as waste, hiring more people to process timber than to cut it, orienting themselves more and more toward manufacturing.

The salmon fishery, while still important to individual communities, was occupying an increasingly minor place in the regional economy. "The salmon fisheries have been important elements in the regional economy in the past, but it seems unlikely that they will retain even their present status in the future," observed the *Harvard Business Review*. "In the 1880s the fisheries provided employment for almost as many persons as did the forest products industries. But the peak in the Pacific Northwest salmon pack was reached in the decade from 1910 to 1919 and has declined since. The decade of the 1930s was only slightly above that of the 1890s, and the present decade will show still lower figures.

"Although the fisheries will continue to be an important part of the economy of the Northwest, they will be of much less relative importance than they were in the past. Much attention must be given to . . . stabilizing the industry."

There were fewer fish, fewer trees, but more manufacturing. There were also more cars, more trucks, better roads, and higher costs for waterborne transportation. Travel around the Sound was done increasingly on land. As it had at the end of World War I, the Puget Sound Navigation Company provided a barometer for the changing transportation patterns.

The company had abandoned its old passenger and freight vessels and now carried both people and cargo on its fleet of ferries, which it operated under the trade name of the Black Ball Line. Traffic on the Black Ball ferries, which tied the islands and the Kitsap Peninsula to the east side of Puget Sound, had expanded tremendously during World War II, chiefly on the run between Seattle and Bremerton. In response to this increased traffic, the company had cut its rates below those of 1937. When the war ended and traffic fell off sharply, the company raised its rates again, first, to the 1937 level and then, at the start of 1947, asking for an increase that would place the rates thirty percent above those of 1937. Considering the increased costs of fuel and labor, that was not totally unreasonable, but the people who depended on ferries were outraged. Their communities couldn't survive economically without ferries, and they had always counted on ferry transportation being cheap. On Vashon, the Chamber of Commerce quickly hired an attorney to fight the fare increase. In Kitsap County, the South Kitsap Improvement Council began pushing for bridges from Seattle to Vashon to the Peninsula. The Vashon people, with their attorney, went to the state capitol where they introduced a bill that would allow people to form their own ferry districts and to operate their own boats.

People who depended on ferries were mobilizing all around the Sound. On Vashon, a mass meeting at the high school raised fifteen hundred dollars for the fight. The local reporter who covered the meeting noted that "Massa Mukai, speaking on behalf of Island farmers, pointed out that the proposed increase in rates would mean a big boost in costs to the farmer, not only in supplies received from the mainland, but also in produce and goods shipped off the island. . . .

"Ferguson Beall [a greenhouse operator], representing Island businessmen, voiced outspoken opposition to the ferry company's demands."

In February, representatives of communities around the Sound that were affected by the fare increase met in Seattle. The president of the Puget Sound Navigation Company, Captain Alex M. Peabody, showed up unexpectedly and told the crowd that auto traffic had increased, forcing him to expand service, while passenger traffic had decreased so much that total revenues had dropped. When Peabody finished, the president of the Vashon Businessmen's Club suggested that "Puget Sound seems to have outgrown the Puget Sound Navigation Company."

A week later, irate ferry riders from all around the Sound joined automobile "caravans" to Olympia, where they asked to have the rate increase postponed.

People felt that Peabody was using his monopoly position to gouge them. "The Black Ball president uses exactly the same arguments now, after five years of fantastically good business, that he used in 1937, after seven years of acute depression," observed one letter to the editor.

In May 1947, the bill allowing the formation of ferry districts was passed by the state legislature. In September, despite bad weather and a light turnout, Vashon voters made their island into a ferry district by a margin of almost ten to one.

The following March, when Peabody interrupted his regular ferry service, the Vashon ferry district kept a boat running. Peabody gave up his charter from the state and contracted individually with county governments, which left him free from state control. He then jacked rates to an average of sixty-nine percent above the 1937 level. Commuters organized the Puget Sound Ferry Users Association to fight both the high rates and Peabody's monopoly.

The Vashon Chamber of Commerce asked for a bridge to the Kitsap Peninsula as part of a whole system of bridges on the Sound. Groups in Kitsap County were still pushing for bridges, too. They felt themselves growing increasingly isolated. Regular ferry service was needed for immediate survival, but it held out few prospects for growth. In an automobile-centered society, ferries would never be a fully satisfactory commercial link.

On August 17, 1948, the *Seattle Post-Intelligencer* announced in a front-page headline, "Black Ball 'Offer' to Sell Ferries Accepted by State." The article beneath the headline showed clearly how confused the situation was. "The State Toll Bridge Authority voted last night to accept what Governor Mon C. Wallgren termed the Puget Sound Navigation Company's offer to sell its properties for $5,975,000," the paper said.

"Meanwhile, in Seattle, Captain Alex M. Peabody, president of the company, asserted flatly: 'I know nothing about such an offer.' "

That day, the governor announced that the company had agreed to sell. "The governor also announced," the *Post-Intelligencer* reported, "that the state will call for bids to build the Agate Pass Bridge," connecting the Peninsula to Bainbridge Island—a step that Peabody himself had long advocated as a means of cutting out unprofitable ferry runs and channeling more people onto the heavily used ferries between Seattle and both Bremerton and the east side of Bainbridge. "The ferry rates at the outset of state operation would average about 50 per cent above the 1937 schedule," the paper noted. "The Governor . . . pointed out . . . that the rate can be lowered . . . upon completion of the Agate Pass Bridge. This would be made possible by consolidation and elimination of unprofitable routes." In other words, while Peabody was trying to gouge the public, no one was going to make money serving his routes at pre-war prices.

The fleet that the state envisioned buying consisted of twenty-one vessels, the two newest of which had been built in 1930, the oldest in 1900. Twelve were steel, the rest wood. Six, all wooden, had been built around Puget Sound, three at Houghton on Lake Washington, and one each at Dockton, Gig Harbor, and Winslow.

The Seattle Metal Trades Council unanimously passed a resolution introduced by Electrician's Union local 46 condemning the proposed purchase on the ground that the fleet was obsolete and that the state would be better advised to build a completely new fleet—in Puget Sound shipyards, of course. Just as at the end of World War I, the shipyard unions were eager to regain their wartime prosperity, and painfully aware that it could not be regained. In August, a federal maritime commission member, Joseph K. Carson, had told a meeting of Puget Sound area shipping-industry and union representatives that the chances of local yards getting government contracts in the foreseeable future were slim. "There is going to be some ship construction," he said, "but the maritime commission is bound by law to award all such contracts to the lowest bidders."

When Captain Alex Peabody sold out to the state, he sold only the passenger franchise, keeping the right to operate freight boats on Puget Sound, and also keeping two ferries.

One ferry was taken north, given Canadian registry, and operated along the coast of British Columbia by Black Ball of Canada, Ltd. The other ferry and the right to operate freight boats were sold to a newly formed subsidiary of the Black Ball Freight Service called Black Ball Transport. Black Ball Transport stopped running freight boats in 1970, but it still operates a ferry between Port Angeles and Victoria.

Below: In 1948, when the Black Ball line protested state denial of a fare increase, ferries were halted for eight days (Seattle Times photo).

Those low bidders weren't likely to be on Puget Sound, where expensive labor and transportation still kept shipbuilding costs higher than they were in other regions. Nor was the state likely to bail the shipyards out with fat ferry contracts.

The union leaders weren't the only people who attacked Wallgren's proposed purchase. The whole situation was quickly incorporated into the electoral politics of 1948.

"It is evident that the whole deal which puts the state willy-nilly into the ferry business is being conducted with one eye on the September 14 primary and the other eye on the November 2 final election," a *Post-Intelligencer* editorial said. "First the governor told us Henry Kaiser was to build a great fleet of fast new ferries to replace the Black Ball Line. But of course not in shipyards in this state. We couldn't build them fast enough or good enough.

"Next we learned it had been decided Puget Sound shipyards could build the ferries after all. (This developed a few days after a prompt outcry from shipyard unions and other civic organizations interested in maintaining and developing industry within the state.) . . .

"Plans were to be rushed for a peninsula bridge . . . [and] a series of other bridges. . . .

"Later the *Post-Intelligencer* discovered by persistent digging at Olympia and in Chicago that the state administration was secretly negotiating for purchase of the Black Ball ferries. . . .

"The *Post-Intelligencer* deeply sympathizes with the plight of island and peninsula residents attempting to cope with mounting transportation costs which discourage cross-sound traffic.

"And there are good and plausible arguments that the state should operate the ferries as part of the highway system to allow orderly development of that rich portion of the state which lies on the islands and the western slopes of Puget Sound.

"But . . . let us divorce it so far as possible from the frantic politics with which the state is now being plunged into a dubious business venture with warmed-over ferry rates which are scarcely distinguishable from those now in effect."

Needless to say, the deal was not divorced from politics at all. Wallgren's gubernatorial opponent, Arthur Langlie, quickly condemned the secrecy of the negotiations and the high price being proposed for Peabody's aging fleet. The deal went through. Langlie was elected. The state supreme court declared the purchase unconstitutional. The situation remained in legal limbo until the spring of 1951, but it was clear from 1948 that the ferry system would eventually be run by the state.

The purchase finally went through on May 31, 1951. The following week, the Vashon paper noted that "Vashon Island merchants reported the heaviest Sunday business ever, due to the improved ferry schedule and an influx of visitors."

That quick surge of weekend business was not really an indication of things to come. At the end of the war, it had seemed that state operation of the ferry system might put the islands and peninsula towns back in the mainstream of commerce, as they once had been. When Wallgren first announced the purchase of the Black Ball fleet, the president of the Ferry Users' Association, Karl Kaye, said it would be "a great stride in the development of the entire state."

He explained that in addition to bringing "a revival of the tourist business, a great factor in itself, increased ferry traffic . . . will be a great commercial attraction. . . .

"As things stand now there are approximately 125,000 people on the Olympic Peninsula who have no access to Eastern Washington markets because trucks, automobiles and individuals are prohibited by high rates from crossing Puget Sound to reach the east side, and the east side finds it out of the question to get to the Olympic Peninsula."

By 1951, it was clear that state ownership would not bring back cheap water transportation and that routes which used the Sound would never be as attractive to shippers as routes that were entirely overland.

A year before the state took over, Langlie, in words reminiscent of Kaye's, noted that the west side of the Sound "has vast potentialities for development. It is rich in timber resources, forest product manufacturing, dairying and agriculture. It has great natural beauty and provides many of our most popular tourist attractions." Langlie, however, didn't suggest that a state-owned ferry system would or could open the western shore of the Sound to substantial development. Instead, he said that "no fully satisfactory answer to the transportation needs of the Puget Sound area will be accomplished until this magnificent body of water is adequately bridged." The "magnificent body of water" was now in the way. For local transportation, the society around it was oriented irrevocably toward the land.

On the state's first day in the ferry business, Langlie told a Seattle Chamber of Commerce luncheon that state operation of ferries was simply a first step toward the construction of bridges. Earlier in the year, the Vashon Chamber of Commerce had resolved to increase its efforts to get bridges built. The bridge at Agate Pass did get built, as did one across the mouth of Hood Canal. A bridge across the Tacoma Narrows, built in the 1930s but soon blown down by a high wind, was replaced. (The Hood Canal bridge sank in a storm in 1979.) Those turned out to be all the bridges built on Puget Sound. None was built to a center of industrial or population growth, and none had as much social or economic impact as did the bridges built east from Seattle across

Right: On November 7, 1940, the Tacoma Narrows bridge collapsed—five months after opening. Below: The present bridge across the Tacoma Narrows (HPCUW, Farquharson photos).

Lake Washington. The latter allowed the city's population to spread inland, where there was a lot of flat, relatively cheap farm and timberland. When suburbanization hit the Puget Sound region, as it hit the rest of the United States in the 1950s and 1960s, the center of population moved back from the water, making proximity to the Sound less a fact of daily life than an amenity for an increasing number of people.

The whole drawn-out saga of the ferry system proved beyond a shadow of a doubt that Puget Sound no longer was and never again would be a cheap local highway. Ferry users could protest as bitterly as they liked, but the fact remained that no other private company had offered to run the ferries at rates lower than the old Black Ball Line demanded, and even the state wasn't willing to run them for much less. The water itself still cost nothing, but operating a boat was increasingly expensive. Highways and bridges cost a great deal, but driving on them was cheap. Businesses that depended entirely on ferry service would have to live with higher costs. Small communities that depended on water transportation would find themselves more and more isolated.

*The hydraulic power block was first demonstrated by MARCO
at Seattle's Fishermen's Terminal (MARCO)*

economic rationality
had nothing to do with it

If private enterprise was bailing out of the business of operating old boats between small communities on Puget Sound, individual fisherman were taking to the water in greater numbers with equipment more elaborate and expensive than ever before. The economic efficiency of small boats remained low, but the technology available to the operators of those small boats changed radically after the war. The ten-and-one-half-ton marine diesel engine in the purse seiner *Janet G.* was exactly twenty years old in 1949. Although it still ran well, it was pulled out and replaced with a new marine diesel—which was more powerful and weighed only as much as the flywheel of the old engine.

Starting around 1951, nylon nets became available, and gillnetters started trading in their old linen nets. Unlike the linen, the nylon wouldn't rot if left wet on the deck, didn't have to be washed regularly with "bluestone"—i.e., copper sulfate—to keep bacteria down. Observers estimated that nylon nets doubled the efficiency of a gillnetter. The number of gillnet boats also increased. In 1944, the year work began to route fish around the Hells Gate rockslide, some fifty-five gillnetters fished on the Fraser River sockeye run. The next year, there were only forty-six. By 1952 and 1953, the numbers increased to 192 and 322. By 1956, there were 491 boats, and by 1957, there were 637.

The purse seine fleet, which required larger crews and larger capital investments, grew much less rapidly. Still, in the dozen years after the end of World War II, the number of purse seiners grew by roughly one-half.

The technology of purse seining improved dramatically. After the early 1950s, the jobs that had always been done by sheer muscle power, or muscle power aided only by simple pulleys, were done increasingly by hydraulics.

The most important invention from the view of the men who had spent their working lives hauling fish-laden seine nets out of the water was the "power block." The block used hydraulics to hoist netfuls of fish to the boom above the deck. It doubled or tripled the number of times a seiner could set its nets each day, and, simultaneously, Robert J. Browning writes in *Fisheries of the North Pacific,* "removed salmon

seiner crewmen from their status as the successors to the galley slave."
It was a creation of a Yugoslavian immigrant named Mario Puretic.

"Before Puretic and his Power Block," Browning observes, "it took
eight to 10 men to work a salmon seine. It was work of the hardest
kind."

Puretic had seined for mackerel, anchovies, and sardines in the
ocean off southern California and had decided that there must be an
alternative to human muscle power for hauling seine nets out of the water. In 1954, he came up with the idea of the power block. He tried it
successfully on a San Pedro fishing boat, but other southern California
fishermen weren't interested. " 'The news travelled fast,' " however,
Puretic wrote to Browning in 1969, and early in 1955, " 'small groups
of fishermen from Puget Sound and British Columbia flew down to San
Pedro to see what they couldn't believe. When they returned home,
they gave MARCO [the Marine Construction and Design Company of
Seattle] my address and immediately MARCO wrote me, inviting me to
Seattle. . . . I came to Seattle with the prototype Power Block in the
trunk of my car.' "

"While Peter Schmidt [founder and president of MARCO] and
Puretic put together a financial agreement," Browning writes,
"MARCO engineers began to plan for production of the Power Block.
The prototype 'was suspended on top of the boom on the salmon boat
Bullmoose and, as the fishermen observed the performance, MARCO
was taking hundreds of orders even before the Power Block was put on
the drafting board.' . . . ''

"So many seiner men wanted the Power Block 'right now' that
MARCO had to assign numbers to impatient skippers on a first-come
first-served basis. . . . That was 1955. By 1960 a skipper in the northern
seine fleets who could not boast a Power Block was regarded as something of a poor relation. . . .''

"From the MARCO yard on Salmon Bay in Seattle, the Power
Block has swept around the world. Modifications of it are used in every
major seine fishery. By 1972, well more than 11,000 Power Blocks were
in use in 40 or more countries."

In Puget Sound, the new fishing technology was being aimed at
salmon runs that in some cases had recovered from their absolute na-
dirs but had never regained the record levels of decades past. The fish
were being spread ever more thinly among the fishermen and boats.
Only a steep increase in the price of salmon—the fish's elevation from
a staple to a luxury—made it economically feasible for all those boats
to stay out on the water. Even so, many fishermen were making little, if
any, profit, and the problems of managing the fishery were becoming
increasingly complex. During the mid-1950s, some Puget Sound gillnetters started going into the open ocean, entirely beyond the limits of

state jurisdiction. They caught lots of fish—some boats regularly hauled in more than a ton a day—but they fell afoul of international politics. After World War II, big Japanese boats started catching salmon in the mid-Pacific; a treaty forced on Japan by the United States and Canada kept those boats west of 175 degrees west longitude, but their mile-long gillnets still managed to catch salmon spawned in Alaska. The U.S. government, wanting to stop the Japanese from catching American salmon, argued that all high-seas net fishing for salmon was biologically unwise and should be banned. In order to make that argument plausible, the government had to ban high-seas net fishing by its own citizens, too. So, the adventurous gillnetters were out of luck. If they had been allowed to continue fishing on the open ocean, state management of the salmon runs might have become physically impossible. Within the enclosed waters of the Sound the physical problems were bad enough, and the economic and political problems were even worse.

In 1957, Thomas Reid, chairman of the International Pacific Salmon Fisheries Commission, complained that "the only action the Commission can take to offset the effects of the rapid increase in fishing efficiency and fleet size is to reduce fishing time." The fishing time was already so short, he said, that it was impossible to make sure the catch was being divided evenly between Americans and Canadians, impossible to be sure that enough fish were getting up the river to spawn. (By then, thanks largely to the efforts of Canada's Minister of Fisheries, James Sinclair, the I.P.S.F.C. was managing pink salmon from the Fraser River, as well as sockeye.) With such short work weeks, fishing might soon become unprofitable. Reid's solution was for the state of Washington to limit the amount of fishing gear on the water. As a means of altering the ratio of fishermen to fish, the suggestion was eminently logical. Politically, it was much too hazardous to touch: state officials weren't about to tell some fishermen they no longer had a right to fish.

The situation didn't improve. At the end of 1961, a new chairman of the Commission, DeWitt Gilbert, said in Bellingham that "the industry generally considers 1961 a disastrous season, despite the fact that it yielded the third largest pack made on this [spawning] cycle since 1917. What is wrong when third-best in 11 cycle years is a 'disaster?' . . . The answer, plainly, lies in over-development of the fishery."

In the 1960s it was ironic that any American coastal fishery could be considered "over-developed." The American fishing industry had been declining ever since the end of World War II, as small American boats lost ground to fleets of bigger, better equipped, more heavily financed foreign vessels. The Japanese ships that caught salmon in the mid-Pacific were only a small part of the foreign competition. During

In the early 1960s, foreign trawlers caught hake off the Washington coast and aroused suspicions— never verified by either direct inspections or aerial photography—that they were also catching salmon (NMFS photo).

Below: Fishermen's Terminal in Seattle, c. 1950 (PSMHS/WC).

the 1960s, fleets of foreign factory ships came to dominate many of the waters along the American coast. Early in the decade, both Japanese and Russian factory ships appeared along the coasts of Washington, Oregon, and California, where they caught hake and other groundfish and aroused suspicions—never verified by either direct inspections or aerial photography—that they were also catching salmon. While foreign governments and quasi-governmental corporations were financing big, highly mechanized fishing vessels, the United States remained committed to the small boat—and to the small entrepreneur who operated it.

Puget Sound was one of the very few places where it was considered necessary to make small fishing boats, in the aggregate, even less efficient. It was a matter of simple arithmetic: unless the number of boats leveled off or decreased, or the number of salmon increased sharply, the catch per boat had to decline. Consequently, fishing periods were made shorter and shorter. This created a lot of resentment and a lot of pressure to consider the short-term economic needs of the fishermen instead of the long-term biological needs of the fish. DeWitt Gilbert observed in 1961 that "local economic pressures . . . make proper escapement safeguards difficult."

A couple of months later, in February 1962, the Washington Governor's Fisheries Advisory Committee recommended that the University of Washington make an economic and management survey of the salmon fishery. A five-man group, headed by the Dean of the University's College of Fisheries, William F. Royce, did the work. In addition to reviewing the available literature, the group took surveys among fishermen and ran numbers through computers.

In February 1963, the group issued its report. Fisheries in which no limit was placed on the number of fishermen or boats "invariably produce low incomes and poor efficiency," it stated right in the introduction. "This problem of excess fishing effort has plagued fishermen and those concerned with the conservation of fish in Washington for many years. It has recently become a much more urgent problem as people realized that they had had years of near record salmon production that were yielding little if any profit to the salmon fisherman. . . .

"Over the past fifteen years we have been using more and more fishing effort to catch fewer and fewer fish. . . .

"It obviously makes no sense to incur greater and greater costs for smaller and smaller catch[es]." It made no sense from society's point of view, that is. For the individual, it would have made no sense only if the price per fish had remained the same. Actually, the price had risen dramatically. The University of Washington group conceded that "in part, the situation simply reflects increases in the prices of salmon in the post-war years, a trend accentuated by the serious decline in salmon production from the major fishery in Alaska. As long as prices continue to climb it is possible to waste large amounts of capital and labor through excessive numbers of fishing units without forcing more than a few fishermen out of the operation."

From an economist's point of view, the seining business obviously wasn't worth the effort. The University of Washington group found that the replacement value of a seine boat and its accessories was about $77,000 and that "the expected rate of return on the investment required for a replacement purse seiner would be somewhat lower than the rate of return that could be earned from a savings and loan account."

Gillnetting struck the group as even more appalling. "For the years 1959-1961 total taxable income from all sources reported by the surveyed group [of gillnetters] averaged only $5,560," the members wrote. "Gross incomes from Puget Sound fishing averaged $2,324 for the odd years 1959 and 1961, and only $1,711 in 1960, when no pink salmon were available. Net returns averaged less than half these amounts.

"The casual nature of the gill net fishery, with its emphasis on part-time operation, is clearly indicated by the following figures. Twenty-five percent of the respondents obtained some income from other salmon fishing. About 19 percent had some income from other types of fishing, and more than 54 percent earned some income from nonfishing jobs. . . . The number who drew unemployment compensation ranged from 17 percent in 1959 to 25 percent in 1961. . . .

"The evidence is clear that total incomes received by gill netters from all sources are slightly below the average incomes for all Washington residents, despite an investment of $6,000 to $7,000 in boat and gear. . . ."

Seiner crewmen were even worse off—"It is impossible to earn, in purse seine fishing, even half of the average income received by all Washington State residents," the group reported. "The principal outside job indicated by respondents was longshoring, which is even more erratic as a source of income. . . .

"If a man wishes to fish during the summer, he removes himself from most regular employment and has great difficulty in finding other part-time work during the winter. . . . respondents drew unemployment compensation in 59 percent of the man-years reported."

Within an economist's frame of reference, commercial salmon fishing had become a totally irrational way to earn one's living. But that frame of reference was very narrow. The University committee was analyzing the industry as if owning or working on a fishing boat was the same as owning or working in a grocery store. From a statistical point of view, it may have been. From a psychological point of view, it wasn't. The fisherman earned his perhaps paltry income for an extremely short working year. Salmon fishing had always, by its very nature, been a seasonal occupation, and the people who chose it had always accepted the need to do something else or the opportunity to do nothing during the off-season. They had also chosen this occupation—or stayed with it—for much the same reason that people had chosen or stayed in small-scale farming: it wasn't just a way to make a living, it was a way of life.

For any given fisherman, therefore, the economic arguments may have been largely beside the point. For the fishing industry as a whole—viewed as an economic entity, not a collective regional life-style—they were right on target. More boats with better gear were chasing fewer fish, and on the average, they weren't making much money doing it. Economically, the system was absurd. The economists on the committee thought it should be changed, and their idea of how to change it was exactly what one might have expected: reduce the amount of commercial fishing gear in Puget Sound—by one-third—so that every fisherman who was left could reap a decent return on his investment and labor. Specific recommendations were to freeze the amount of gear at the level then current, raise license fees, and use the money to buy back the boats of fishermen who were willing to retire.

The economic logic of their recommendations was irrefutable and was accepted by some of the commercial fishermen. However, the economic logic conflicted sharply with the social and political logic of giving everyone an equal chance to catch salmon. The conflict was particularly sharp in the depressed regional economy of the mid-1960s, but it persisted even after times improved. The fishery had always been open to everyone. The skilled fisherman would virtually always wind up catching more fish than the unskilled, but after Initiative 77 abolished the fish traps, no one was permitted to use gear efficient enough to take a great many more fish than his neighbor. Economic logic led squarely back to fish traps, if one wanted to follow it far enough. Even without following it quite that far, one would inevitably reach a point at which some citizens would have access to the public salmon in the public waters of the Sound and others wouldn't. That prospect didn't appeal to state officials, who didn't take the idea of "limited entry" into the fishery very far. It didn't appeal very strongly to the fishermen, either. Instead of pushing for the establishment of a limited entry system, they devoted most of their political energy to squabbling among themselves, each trying to get some advantage for his own particular kind of fishing gear. Smart economists might stand on the sidelines and say it was all ridiculous—some smart economists did—but no one else wanted to take responsibility for excluding his fellow citizens from the salmon fishery, denying them access to what had always been a way of life open to all. Economic rationality had nothing to do with it.

Digesters, under construction, prior to being encased in concrete.
Sulphite digesters "cook" wood chips down to pulp (NREPL, Juleen photo)

free to dump anything

The salmon fishing industry showed so little enthusiasm for internal reform partly because each group of fishermen had so many tempting external targets. U.S. Senator Slade Gorton recalls that when he went to Olympia as a freshman legislator in 1958, he was shocked by the intensity of feeling that he found among representatives of fishermen's groups. "The emotions were strong," he recalls, and they radiated out in all directions. "It was the commercial fishermen against the sport fishermen, the gillnetters against the trollers against the seiners, and all the fishing groups against the pulp mills, which of course at that time were free to dump anything they liked (into the Sound)."

Pulp mills had long since become regional symbols of pollution. By 1958, the pulp industry on Puget Sound was some three decades old. Fishermen who had watched it develop felt strongly that the industry had destroyed more salmon than any other single institution on the Sound. The mills at Everett were widely credited with wiping out most of the Snohomish and Stillaguamish river runs. Old fishermen can still remember that around the Everett harbor, "for 10 or 15 years, nobody even bothered copper-painting their boats," because destructive organisms couldn't survive in the polluted water.

Sport fishermen were equally sure that the mills didn't do marine life any good. The oystermen, of course, had been sure since the late 1920s. Still, it had been virtually impossible to do anything about the mills. The political power wielded by Reed and the pulp industry's other partisans was only part of the problem. Even many people who detested pulp mills saw no way to combat them. How could the mills operate without discharging wastes? If the mills couldn't operate, what would happen to all those jobs? It was hard to figure out what to do, hard even to make a convincing gesture.

Actually, however frustrating the situation may have been, a foundation for political action was being laid—in large part by the mills themselves, which were making people aware of the environmental problems and providing a focus for the bare beginnings of a political movement. It's difficult to figure out exactly when or how an anti-pollution movement in the Puget Sound area began. The oystermen were primarily responsible for having the first local studies of pollution damage made and for making pollution at least a limited public issue. However, if Ken McLeod's memory is accurate, the person primarily responsible for starting a broadly based anti-pollution movement was not an oysterman but a Seattle sport fisherman named Don Johnson who founded the Washington State Sportmen's Council.

As McLeod remembers, it was Johnson and he who drafted and got passed—albeit in watered-down form—the bill that established the state's first independent pollution control board. R. H. Bailey, an oysterman with beds in Padilla Bay, who sued the Bellingham pulp mill unsuccessfully in 1939, claimed in the 1960s that he himself had fathered the bill. Whoever was responsible, the bill passed in 1945.

It was a landmark, but it had little impact on the major pollution problems of the Sound. From time to time during the next decade, a state inspector might force a gravel pit to stop sluicing dirt directly into a trout stream, but he wasn't going to shut down a pulp mill.

For a while in the late 1940s, that seemed almost beside the point; the concerns over pulp mills seemed—at least to some observers—to have passed largely into history. A Pollution Control Commission progress report observed in 1947 that while in the Oakland Bay area near Shelton, "complaints and suits from oyster growers practically forced the local mill to close before the war," the situation had improved dramatically. The mill had closed down temporarily during the early years of World War II. "Before the mill was reopened in 1944 a new cooking base (ammonia) was decided upon" and using the new base, almost all the concentrated sulfite waste could be evaporated. As a result, "the commercial oyster beds in Oakland Bay and the Narrows . . . are no longer adversely affected . . . [and] oyster production is on the upgrade."

In Bellingham, the report said, the Puget Sound Pulp and Timber Company had installed an alcohol recovery plant and other equipment that had reduced the volume of waste by one-half. "Before the war the oyster growers of Samish Bay from 6–10 miles from the pulp mill brought suit for damage to their oyster . . . crops. Since the alcohol plant was started, there has been no more contention between the oyster growers and the pulp mill."

It looked as though technology might have accomplished what political action had not. The optimism was short-lived, though. In 1935, some eight years after pulp mill pollution had started cutting into oyster yields, the harvest of Olympia oysters had been 319,900 pounds. By 1956, the annual harvest had dropped to 31,884 pounds. Oystermen still believed the mills were largely responsible.

"The North Sound Oyster industry is about completely shut down," R. H. Bailey told the Pollution Control Commission in 1958. During the 1930s, Bailey had built up a lucrative business processing a product called Bailey's Oyster Soup and had operated a plant on the Everett waterfront that was billed as the largest oyster cannery in the world. He also had oyster beds in Samish Bay and took scowloads of oysters from Port Susan, north of Everett. Bailey believed that pollution from the mills in Bellingham and Everett had wiped out the oyster beds in both places, and he had become a crusader for clean water.

He told the Pollution Control Commission that pulp mill pollution was worse than ever. It had seemed to disappear partly because, during the war, there had been an emphasis on producing lumber rather than pulp. Controls had been installed, but they had been more than offset by postwar increases in production. In Bellingham, the mill had indeed spent three million dollars on by-product plants that reduced its rate of sulfite emission by ten percent. However, it had also doubled the capacity of the plant. The net result was an eighty percent increase in the volume of pulp liquor emitted.

If the commission thought otherwise, it should look for itself, Bailey said, not trust the water sampling done by the pulp mills. In the past, he said, "samples have been taken by the pulp mill crew . . . from alongside a moving boat where the wake has thrown the sulphite liquor well away. No wonder they got little or no liquor in their samples."

The pollution fight by then was no longer the exclusive property of Bailey or the oystermen. In fact, sportsmen who were active at the time don't remember the oystermen *per se* playing a significant part. That may be largely a matter of perspective. Certainly, the oystermen were no closer than ever to creating a wider constituency.

Bailey himself had finally managed to put the situation in a broader perspective. In 1958, speaking to the state Pollution Control Commission in Bellingham, he cast it in terms that were familiar from the fight over fish traps, terms that would become even more familiar in the decades ahead. The real question, he said, was whether the use of the public water by one large industry would make other uses by other people impossible.

"The people of Bellingham . . . are too close to the picture to realize that they could and should have the pulp mill and also clean water," he said. Historically, no single use had excluded any other. In 1912, when he first visited the area, "Bellingham was a picture with its sawmills, fish traps and canneries. We had multiple use of Bellingham Bay waters. The sawmills burned most of their waste, but some escaped into the bay. There was a slight discoloration of water around the log booms. Some cannery offal went into the water and made food for the fish and crabs. Even domestic sewage after its initial oxygen demand is satisfactory because [it is] a fertilizer for plankton growth which feeds the small fish—which, in turn, are food for the big fish. *That was multiple use of the water.*

"The pulp mill was built in 1926 and had a capacity of 22 tons per day. Capacity doubled the next year and many times thereafter until it is now 20 times its original size. The pulp mill was a new breed of cat. . . . today we have no multiple use of the water—*we have an absolute monopoly of its use by the pulp mill.*"

At first, public interest focused less on who was dumping wastes into the Sound than on what was being dumped. The federal government had helped to stimulate the interest in 1951, by issuing a report which indicated that the Sound was the sixth most polluted area in the country. One could still see the trees and mountains around the shore, still pull salmon from the waters, but those waters had become less than pristine.

In the early 1950s, a sport fisherman named Tom Wimmer decided that state permits should be required for the dumping of wastes into public waters. He, attorney Irving Clark, and two other sportsmen took a permit bill to the state legislature. Oyster growers and commercial fishermen were very hostile to the proposed legislation. They said a state permit for dumping wastes would simply be a "license to pollute." They were right, after a fashion, but Wimmer maintained that the public would be better off if the state at least knew what kind of and how much waste each industrial plant was dumping into the Sound. He, Clark, and their colleagues persisted. The legislation passed in 1955.

That same year, a young University of Washington limnologist, George Anderson, went sailing on Lake Washington, east of Seattle, and thought the water looked somehow *different.* He took a sample in an empty beer bottle; when he returned to his laboratory, he looked at the sample under a microscope. In the sample, he found an organism named *Oscillatoria rubescens,* which had been instrumental in causing the "death" of several similar lakes in Switzerland. It was already obvious that treated sewage from communities around the lake was starting to pollute the water, just as it was obvious that the raw Seattle sewage pouring into Elliott Bay was making the water there unfit for swimming. Until the mid-1950s, there was no particular public pressure to do anything about the water pollution. The small communities around Lake Washington had started treating their sewage in the 1930s so that it wouldn't be a health hazard, but that had only speeded up the growth of algae in the lake. Those same communities had neither the will nor the resources nor the necessary sense of direction to do anything more.

At around the time that *Oscillatoria rubescens* showed up in the lake, a young Seattle attorney named James Ellis came up with a plan for saving the lake: build a big sewer line all the way around the lake, and run the sewage first through a treatment plant and then out into the Sound; form a quasi-governmental organization that could oversee construction and operation of the system, and issue bonds and levy service charges to pay for it. Ellis and his colleagues prepared a bill, which was introduced by a first-term representative named Daniel Evans and was passed by the legislature in 1956. The legislation allowed the plan to be put up to a vote of the people in the area within which the new organization (to be known as the Municipality of Metropolitan Seattle) would function. Originally, the organization, commonly called METRO, was to handle not only sewage, but also transportation and planning. In March 1958, the measure won a majority but lost under a complicated system of weighting votes. In September, with transportation and planning dropped from the proposal, it passed. The METRO project was the first major commitment to fighting pollution made in any metropolitan area in the United States. Within a dozen years, Lake Washington was as clear as it had been in 1950.

The pollution involved was a result of municipal sewage disposal, however. It was not the waste discharged by a powerful industry. As Ellis recalled later, "It's easy to make people feel guilty if they vote against a pollution measure. You can talk to them about fouling their own nest. It's easy to dramatize." Industrial pollution was, at the time, quite another story.

"Since the first commercial sulphite pulp mill operation was founded, fishermen have owlishly eyed the immense plants and the resultant 'belly-up' salmon which have lined streams and harbors," observed the Fishermen's News of September 5, 1957. "Up until 1942, when the Weyerhaeuser Timber Company developed the magnesium oxide process, the mills legitimately argued that there was no known method of reducing or eliminating pulp liquor pollution without shutting down the mills. Fishermen and oyster operators agreed that closure was not the answer and encouraged the search for a means whereby both fish and pulp liquors could exist harmoniously.

"Today, however, fishermen and oystermen are something less than pleased to hear the same argument. . . .

Milo Moore, newly-appointed Washington Director of Fisheries . . . recently accused [Virgil] Bacon, pulp and paper public relations director of 'brainwashing.' . . .

"Nard Jones, Seattle Post-Intelligencer editorial writer, quickly rose to the pulp industry's defense, labeling Moore's statements as 'rude and uncalled for.' . . .

"Mayor Hert Rotter of Shelton, seeing the Rayonier pulp plant in his community shut down [by the management, not the state], sent out the following plea to mayors of cities where pulp mills are in operation: . . . 'The Rayonier pulp mill, located in our city, has given notice of a shut down for an indefinite period of time, beginning August 9. The closing of the operation here in Shelton will have a far-reaching effect."

Cleaning up Lake Washington required first the support of regional voters and later miles of municipal sewage lines laid around the Lake and emptying into Puget Sound (METRO)

The economy of your community and many others in our state may be facing the same problem.' "

The real problem was that with pulp supply exceeding demand, outmoded mills had little economic future. Rotter was implying, though, that if the state stopped pushing the Shelton mill to reduce its sulfite emissions, all would be well again. The pressures of the marketplace didn't count.

" 'By uniting our efforts,' " he said, " 'we can help to assure steady payrolls. . . . The obtaining of a permanent permit from the Pollution Board is of prime importance to every pulp mill in our state. It has been suggested that, as mayors, we combine our efforts to obtain assurance that such permits . . . will be granted.'

"It must have been a bit difficult," the *Fishermen's News* contended, ". . . for Shelton Rayonier manager, Winston Scott, to have shared in any such suggestion in light of his statement to employees July 9 regarding the shutdown.

"At that time, Scott stressed that the shutdown . . . was for an indefinite period because of poor market conditions. . . .

"From July 9, the shutdown turns from a 'market problem' to the need for a 'permanent pollution dumping permit' on July 28. . . .

"Let the pulp industry consider the fishing industry as 'discourteous' but perhaps the enforcement of the laws of the state of Washington citizens requires a certain degree of 'rudeness.' "

As it happened, Rayonier received a five-year dumping permit in 1957, but the mill remained closed.

At around the same time, Bailey and E. J. Gruble of the Puget Sound Oyster Growers said in a letter to the *Post-Intelligencer* that "Puget Sound has almost become a 'marine desert.' . . .

"Seventy-five per cent of the raw liquor still goes directly into Bellingham Bay, and the bay for a considerable distance from the pulp mill is black as ink.

"Pulp mills have wrecked the Skagit County oyster industry."

A few months later, the *Post-Intelligencer* reported that Erik Ekholm of the Puget Sound Pulp and Timber Company of Bellingham contended the waste material dumped into salt water by his plant was not harmful to shellfish.

"Ekholm claimed there is no definite proof of what constitutes pollution harmful to oysters."

Ekholm was echoing Mark Reed's arguments of nearly thirty years before.

The arguments still were—and are to this day—technically correct. In the laboratory, pulp mill effluent had been proven harmful to oysters. In the field, it had not. In a large and complex body of water such as Puget Sound, it is extremely difficult to *prove* that a certain type of pollution has a certain biological effect, and despite decades of study, no one has ever established a clear cause-and-effect relationship between pulp mill effluent and the decline of oyster populations. The circumstantial evidence—the mill starts up, the oyster population declines—had, of course, been striking. Most oystermen found it totally convincing. Still, there was no hard scientific proof.

The pulp and paper industry did not concede and has not conceded that its mills had anything to do with the decline of the native oyster industry. It is true that the mills never lost a dime in court and that the last and largest suit brought by oyster growers against a mill— *Olympia Oyster Co. v. Rayonier, Inc.*—was simply dismissed by U.S. District Court Judge George Boldt in 1964. Boldt ruled there was "no substantial evidence" that the Shelton pulp mill had caused the deaths of oysters in Oyster Bay or that the mill had violated the terms of its State Water Pollution Control Commission permit to discharge wastes. Fisheries Department officials who worked with shellfish thought Boldt's ruling reflected the skill of Rayonier's lawyers, not the merits of Rayonier's case.

They did not believe, however, that the pulp mills were solely responsible for the decline of the Olympia Oyster industry. In fact, the shutting down of the Shelton mill in 1957 did not revive the industry, indicating possibly that by the late 1950s, other sources of pollution had taken a toll and probably that, for economic reasons, people weren't trying to cultivate the oysters at their former rate. The Olympia oyster industry was labor intensive. Before World War II, it had depended heavily on the cheap labor provided by immigrant Japanese families. The Japanese were interned inland at the beginning of the war, and after the war neither they nor anyone else was eager to resume the old labor at anything approaching the old rates of pay.

During the decade that followed World War II, while the old, shopworn arguments about pulp waste and oysters were circulating once again, a new, wealthy industry was moving into the Sound and demonstrating that if one spent enough money to control pollution, one could, in fact, control it. The oil industry—which, a decade or two later, was not widely considered a guardian of clean water—was starting to build refineries on the upper Sound. Some of the people who had been opposing pulp mill pollution used the refineries as proof that industry could be clean. The scale of the new operations didn't disturb them. In 1958, the Citizens for Clean Water noted in a press release that "our largest new industries, the oil refineries, have eliminated almost 100 per cent of their pollution at a cost of $10,000,000."

The refineries provided more than a good example. They were part of a development that was making pulp mills steadily less important to the overall regional economy. By the late 1950s, it was not the mills or even the whole forest products industry that generated some fifty-eight percent of all manufacturing jobs in the Puget Sound area—it was the Boeing Company. Still, in towns such as Bellingham, Shelton, and Everett, the mill was nearly as important as ever. On a state level, gestures, orders, and even threats might be made in the direction of the pulp industry, but no one was ready yet to shut down the mills.

The State Pollution commission in 1956 gave the mills one year to submit plans for evaporating the pulp liquor. The time limit was extended, renewed in 1961, and never enforced.

If nothing much had changed on a local level, on a national level the political climate was quite different by the early 1960s. Eisenhower had been replaced by Kennedy, civil rights was capturing the nation's attention, and federal activism was beginning to spread. Local problems that offended a wider geographical conscience might no longer be dealt with at local discretion. Also, that wider geographical conscience was beginning to take note of the natural environment. In 1961, the first year of Kennedy's term, Congress passed a Federal Water Pollution Control Act that empowered the federal government to help any state with pollution problems if the governor of that state asked for help. In November of the same year, Washington Governor Albert Rosellini wrote to Secretary of Health, Education and Welfare Abraham Ribicoff asking for assistance with the pulp mill problem; a joint state-federal conference was quickly scheduled to be held in Olympia in mid-January. Before the conference, on January 1, the state Pollution Control Commission gave the seven most polluting mills exactly one year to propose alternatives to their current means of waste disposal and three months beyond that in which to submit engineering plans.

On the fourteenth, Assistant Secretary of Health, Education and Welfare James M. Creigley arrived early for the conference, took a ninety-minute plane ride over the Sound, and started making statements to the press about the visible signs of pollution.

The conference led to a decision that the deadlines for the main polluting mills should be extended until July 1962 and January 1963 and that the Pollution Control Commission should proceed under Washington law to develop a control plan.

The industry's defenders were more than a little upset. "On this page today is a letter from a Port Angeles business leader who asks, 'Why does the State Pollution Commission have to harass our Port Angeles pulp and paper mills?' " the Seattle Post-Intelligencer said in its 1962 lead editorial of January 23.

" 'Harass' is the right word. . . ." the editorial concluded.

"The fact that the economic health of Bellingham and other Puget Sound cities depends heavily on the manufacture of pulp and paper does not mean that this or any industry should be immune from public responsibility," began the *Bellingham Herald*, striking a statesmanlike pose.

"Nor do they ask or desire such immunity. . . .

"But the pulp industry . . . does deserve to be free from unwarranted harassment. . . .

"If it were clearly demonstrated that unreasonable pollution detrimental to the fisheries resource or the public health is resulting . . . a cleanup order would be justified. But there is not such proof. . . .

"What constitutes excessive or unjustifiable pollution?"

The sentiments were familiar. For the industry's defenders, no conceivable amount of pollution was ever unjustifiable. What the presence of the federal government signaled was that such local calculations, and the local economics from which they sprang, were no longer the only considerations. From then on—haltingly at first, but inexorably—local sources of pollution were going to be viewed in a broader context. Appeals to local self-determination were inevitable.

The federal government made a convenient scapegoat, and Congressman Jack Westland, whose district included both Everett and Bellingham, was quick to make use of it. "There is being demonstrated in my district and the state of Washington the effect of Federal intervention in problems that concern the State and industry alone," Westland told the House of Representatives on March 5, 1962.

"The people of my district and Washington State recognize the seriousness of the situation," he said. "They know what they will lose. . . .

"This . . . action . . . threatens the closure of seven western Washington mills, because the pulp and paper industry cannot bear the financial burden. . . .

"The mills estimate it would cost $75 million. . . . The three mills in my hometown of Everett would have to spend $35 million. . . .

"The pulp and paper companies . . . have . . . complied with every requirement of the State Pollution Control Commission with the exception of the last demand, which requires that 85 per cent of the sulfite liquor be removed. If this effluent is to be removed, there will be no pulp and paper operations and at least 8,000 directly employed in the industry may lose their jobs.

"In my district alone, some 4,600 employees in the mills may find themselves drawing unemployment checks. . . . in 1960 [they] received almost $29,407,000 [from the mills]. . . .

"What would happen to the farmers who sell the raw product—wood—to the mills? What happens to the gyppo logger and the lumber mill operator who sells chips as a by-product?. . . .

"I cannot understand why the federal government is willing to spend . . . reportedly $200,000 a year indefinitely to push the people of my district and my state around."

The truth was, of course, that the governor of his state had formally asked for federal help, and that for at least some of the people, the economic benefits of the mills—which were not necessarily incompatible with some degree of pollution control—had to be weighed against the damage they inflicted on what was perceived as a public resource.

Also, the regional balance of employment had continued to shift. Those eight thousand pulp mill employees still looked like a lot from the perspective of Bellingham and Everett and Port Angeles. From a regional perspective, where they could be compared to the nearly eighty thousand people who worked at Boeing by the early 1960s, their number seemed less impressive.

Other balances were shifting, too. A national environmental movement was starting to gather steam. The next year saw the climax of the Sierra Club's successful fight against the construction of Glen Canyon Dam on the Colorado River—a fight that made Sierra Club president David Brower a national figure and showed that even when the stakes were high, environmental considerations could prevail over economic ones.

The Puget Sound region was anything but isolated from the growth of environmental consciousness. Since the immediate post-war period, recreational boating and saltwater sport fishing had become major pastimes and the bases for significant industries on the Sound. "In recent years sportsmen have approached a million angler trips annually in Washington State, considerably more than half of them within Puget Sound and the Strait of Juan de Fuca," the University of Washington group that studied the salmon fishery reported in 1963. "Between 500,000 and 1,000,000 fish have been taken annually by sportsmen in recent years, about half of which are taken in Puget Sound and the Strait area. . . . sport fishing is now a major state industry."

As the regional economy and the regional population grew more sophisticated, the Sound and the forests were valued increasingly as amenities, as objects of contemplation and settings for avocational activities. People with money and sophistication and a taste for political combat were acquiring a significant stake in the Sound that had nothing to do with pulp production or merchant shipping or the canning of salmon.

The 747, largest passenger jet in history, was built in Boeing's Everett plant (Boeing photos)

images of the future

The sulfurous odor that routinely hung over Everett, Bellingham, Tacoma, and other pulp mill communities was no longer regarded by everyone as "the smell of progress." Even development-oriented economists had begun to question its desirability. "In a region whose most certain long-run economic resource is beauty, blight becomes a vital economic factor," wrote William Bunge in a 1960 study for the state Department of Commerce and Economic Development. "Especially dangerous are slip-shod tourist and residential developments and the odor problems of Tacoma and Everett."

Not only did the traditional smelly pulp mill detract from the views of deep water and high mountains that induced people from the interior of the nation to spend money beside the Sound, but the mill and its visible accessories also looked more and more vestigial. Those rusting buildings emitting sulfurous smoke were not images of the future. Nor were the great piles of logs that stood beside them, patches of bare wood gleaming through breaks in the bark, ridges of splinters jutting out wherever the two cuts of the chain hadn't quite met. Locally, that log pile still meant jobs and income. But regionally, it was somehow archaic. A pile of thick logs waiting to be turned into lumber or pulp was the old Sound. The new was a row of gleaming jets outside a Boeing plant.

In 1915, the mill Weyerhaeuser built at Everett was the biggest in the world and probably the most highly mechanized, a harbinger of new things. Almost exactly fifty years later, Boeing decided to build the largest passenger jet in history, the 747, in Everett, and set up the world's largest factory building to construct it in. The difference in scale between the old Weyerhaeuser mill and the new Boeing plant, the difference in perceived significance between a pile of logs and a giant jet, the difference in employment between any pulp or lumber mill and any Boeing plant was immense.

In the late 1960s, with the 747 in production and hopes for construction of a supersonic passenger plane, the SST, riding high, Boeing's work force topped one hundred thousand. Congress voted down the SST, of course, airline orders declined, Boeing laid off more than half its workers, and the area was plunged into the 1969-1971 aerospace recession. In 1971, regional unemployment hit fifteen percent. When the region emerged from the recession, Boeing was healthier than ever—although it didn't rehire as many people as it had laid off— and the economy as a whole was less dependent on Boeing or on any other single business.

Statistically, the region was also further than ever removed from the raw-material-oriented, quasi-colonial economy of the previous century. Nevertheless, in almost any Puget Sound port of the early 1970s one could see logs stacked for acres, shreds of bark littering the ground around them, the stark booms of a rusting cargo ship rising behind, with mist hanging low over the water and a dim view of a forested shore beyond. The booms and mist and dark background of trees could almost have belonged to any Sound lumber port of the nineteenth century. The raw logs stacked as cargo could almost have belonged to the early 1850s, to the years during which small communities around the Sound derived their only income from selling pilings or hand-squared timbers to San Francisco.

Shipments of logs and pilings had never stopped entirely, but during most of the region's history, ships leaving the cities and the mill towns had carried sawn lumber. That was true through the 1950s and into the 1960s. As late as 1964, some thirty percent of the East Coast's lumber still came from the Northwest. The Port of Olympia was representative. During the 1950s, its main business was supplying the East Coast with sawn lumber and the products of three plywood mills that had been built during the 1920s. The mills, with antiquated machinery and rigid labor contracts, did not survive the 1960s. Neither did the economic conditions that had made it profitable for Olympia to ship lumber to the East. Land transportation became cheaper and more convenient than ever, and as the timber industry invested in the Southeast—going back to the pine forests from which the Douglas fir region had taken supremacy at the turn of the century—sources of supply opened up much closer to markets in the Northeast.

As land transportation grew more attractive, American shipping grew less so. American ships had always cost more to operate than their foreign competitors, and as World War II receded further into history, the price difference increased, as did the selection of relatively cheap foreign-flag vessels to choose from. If one were shipping lumber, one could afford less and less to use American ships. And since the Jones Act required that all cargoes moving between American ports travel on American vessels, the shipment of lumber from Olympia—or from any other Puget Sound port—to the Northeast became increasingly unattractive.

At the same time, Japan's appetite for wood grew enormously. Japan's forests were depleted, her economy booming, her houses traditionally built of wood. There were plenty of Japanese sawmills, so Japan wasn't interested in importing sawn lumber, just logs. The Japanese paid much more for raw logs than American sawmills did. Whole logs started going from Puget Sound to Japan.

In little mill towns near the Sound, small, antiquated sawmills and plywood mills started closing down. Often, the mill was the only accessible source of jobs; when it closed, there might suddenly be more people in the taverns, more aimless pedestrians on the sidewalks, more street fights. It was easy to conclude that by shipping logs to Japan instead of to that silent mill, the region was actually "exporting jobs." Millworkers' unions and some sympathetic congressmen concluded just that.

Weyerhaeuser and the other big companies exporting logs replied that exporting itself created thousands of jobs; the dockworkers' unions agreed. But questions remained: Why not export sawn lumber instead? Why not ship lumber instead of raw logs to Japan? Why not ship it to the East Coast? Transportation to the East Coast was said to be prohibitively expensive, but British Columbia sold lumber there.

British Columbia shipped some of that lumber at subsidized rail rates, but it also sent some to the East Coast by ship. That was an old, old Puget Sound nightmare come true. Even before Washington became a state, it had been obvious to people interested in shipping lumber from the Sound that British Columbia had all the same natural advantages and—given any legal advantage—could become a dangerous competitor for eastern markets. J. W. Robinson recalled in 1919 that when he took the new state constitution to President Benjamin Harrison in 1889, Secretary of State James G. Blaine told Harrison that "the timber of the new State of Washington is its richest asset . . . but unless this nation continues its policy of protection, the forests of British Columbia will greatly reduce the value of the timber."

That particular concern endured, sharpened by the realization that laws designed to protect American shipping made it cheaper to ship lumber from British Columbia than from the ports of Puget Sound. Such laws existed even before World War I. In 1906, D. E. Skinner, president of the San Francisco firm that had acquired the Port Blakely Mill Company from Renton, Holmes, and Company, wrote to E. G. Ames at Port Gamble that "we need and must have" enough ships available to "develop . . . our opportunities on the East Coast." The "surest means" of getting those ships, Skinner suggested, would be to have Congress change the law so that foreign vessels could travel between American ports on the route around Cape Horn. Skinner wanted Chauncey Griggs of the St. Paul and Tacoma Lumber Company to join him in a lobbying effort and feared that Griggs didn't realize quite how important the legislation would be. Griggs's company, located securely at a railroad on the mainland, was oriented toward markets in the Midwest and secondarily toward markets in California. Skinner and Ames, with their mills on Bainbridge Island and the shore of Hood Canal, had a much greater stake in new shipping laws. Nevertheless, Skinner intended to work on Griggs and hoped Ames, too, would "have him realize" the importance of lobbying for new laws.

The laws were not changed until World War I, when American shippers were grateful for any vessels they could find. After the war, when the Jones Act reimposed the traditional ban on using foreign ships for coastwise trade, northwestern port officials complained that ships would be driven north to Vancouver, British Columbia. That did not happen to any significant extent. After World War II, however, as the price difference between American and foreign-flag shipping increased and the fleets of cheap foreign-flag vessels expanded, the Jones Act became more and more of a straitjacket for the lumber industry. When lumber shipped from Vancouver on foreign vessels cost ten dollars less per thousand board feet than lumber shipped from Puget Sound—as it did by the late 1970s—the East Coast ordered its northwestern lumber from Vancouver.

The ships carrying logs to Japan weren't American, though, and there was no obvious reason why they couldn't take finished lumber instead of logs across the Pacific.

The Jones Act did not prevent them from doing so. However, log-exporting companies argued that Japan simply wasn't interested in buying finished lumber. Japan had no desire to put its own sawmills out of business. Also, partly to protect those mills, lumber sizes were not standardized and varied widely from place to place within Japan. American two-by-fours weren't wanted. Not everyone was convinced by these arguments, but they had some substance, and raw logs kept leaving Puget Sound.

Unemployed millworkers weren't the only people who disliked log exports. Even many people who had no connection with the mills resented having "our" logs sent to "the Japs." Some port officials felt uneasy about it, too, but most of them had little choice. Other cargoes were rare. The Port of Olympia spent most of the 1970s developing a plan to turn some of its space into a marina for pleasure boats. In the remaining space, it continued to handle logs. So did virtually all the other small ports in the region. Just as in the early 1850s, it was only raw logs that kept them functioning as commercial ports. They had little else to offer.

By the mid-1970s, Tacoma was something more than a forest products port, but only Seattle was something entirely different. In Seattle, instead of the traditional log pile, the characteristic image was a lot full of forty-foot aluminum boxes and a big, orange gantry crane plucking one of the boxes from the bed of a truck, hoisting it high into the air, lowering it precisely onto the deck of a fast ship, swinging back to get another box. Trucks kept bringing the boxes. Other cranes were loading other ships nearby.

Not all the years after World War II were that busy for the Port of Seattle. By the late 1950s, the Port had sunk deep into the economic doldrums. Endemic waterfront labor trouble in the late 1940s had hurt its image, but that wasn't the only problem. Increasingly, there wasn't enough "backup" warehouse space behind the docks; most cargo had to be stored someplace before it was loaded onto ships or onto the trains or trucks that would carry it inland; there was never enough room on the docks for it. And in Seattle, there often wasn't enough room anywhere else.

In addition, Portland, Seattle's main rival as a general cargo port in the Northwest, had certain natural advantages: Portland could take the wheat shipped by barge down the Columbia and load it onto ships bound for Japan; when the ships returned from Japan, they could carry steel or other products. As the Port of Portland grew on the basis of this natural trade, other cargoes gravitated there, too.

The economics of maritime commerce changed radically in the mid- and late-1960s. In the decade after World War II, several Seattle-based shipping lines began shipping cargo in large boxes to Alaska. The original companies folded rather quickly, and the practice of shipping in boxes was discontinued, with no noticeable lingering influence on Puget Sound or any place else. Independently, on the East Coast, in 1955, the company that became SeaLand began using containers on the run between New York and Puerto Rico. The system was far from an instant success, but by the early 1960s, the people in charge of the Port of Seattle decided it was the wave of the future. "Containerization" appealed to people in other ports, too, but few staked as much on this technology as early as the Port of Seattle.

Instead of working hard to improve its conventional cargo-handling facilities, Seattle, in the mid-1960s, gambled its resources on containers. Container piers were built out into the harbor, big gantry cranes bought. The main prize would obviously be container trade with the Orient, primarily Japan, but there were problems. The Japanese might still prefer to do business in Portland. Beyond that, the Japanese had no container ships of their own. And the streets that led away from the water in the old Japanese port cities were too narrow and winding for container trucks to navigate. This fear about narrow streets recalled the arguments about odd lumber sizes and small Japanese mills.

It wasn't the first time that port officials had been forced to consider the technological limitations of doing business with the Orient. "The Pacific Coast practice of sacking grain is rather amusing to East-

Containerization required
specialized equipment
(Port of Seattle photos)

erners who are used to bulk methods," wrote the Port of Seattle's chief engineer in 1914. But since "Japanese and Chinese ports so far have not provided facilities for receiving grain in bulk . . . all grain shipped to the Orient is in sacks."

Japan eventually learned to handle grain in bulk, and it accommodated container ships, too. Some of the streets in old Japanese ports proved easier for container trucks to negotiate at night, when the traffic was light, but they did prove negotiable.

Before long, Japan had its own container ships. The Japanese minister of transportation, who realized as well as Seattle port officials did that containers were going to be important, got together representatives of six shipping lines that served the Northwest—none generally on speaking terms with any of the others—and persuaded them to purchase three big container vessels. In 1970, the lines chose Seattle as their northwestern port of entry. One reason was that Seattle had taken its gamble at exactly the right time and already had container facilities in place. Another was Puget Sound. Container ships were large, and their competitive advantage was entirely a matter of speed. Portland lay eight hours up the Columbia River along a channel that could be kept deep enough for big vessels only by constant dredging. Seattle lay on water that was deep enough for any ship. So did Tacoma, of course, but Tacoma hadn't gotten a sufficiently early start.

With hindsight, one can say that Seattle had been preparing itself to become a container port for years. A port official recognized in 1914 that "the key to harbor efficiency . . . is the terminal. Great ships must be kept moving. Quick and cheap handling of freight is imperative."

Handling the bulk of the Japanese silk trade, as Seattle did between the world wars, must have driven the lesson home. Silk was a valuable cargo. Shippers wanted to transform it into dollars as quickly as possible. One didn't leave it lying around in warehouses or on docks. One loaded it onto eastbound trains with all possible speed—sometimes within four hours of its arrival in port.

That same speed in transferring cargo from ships to land transportation and vice versa was what container ports were all about.

The container business boomed, taking over world shipping more rapidly than anyone had expected. By the end of 1977, Seattle was the second-busiest container port in the nation, behind only New York, and sixth-busiest in the world. Unlike other old, established American ports, Seattle handled the new container business within its traditional harbor. In New York, containerization, with its demands for huge, open storage yards, moved most of the cargo handling from the traditional piers in Manhattan and Brooklyn across the Hudson River to Elizabeth and Newark, New Jersey. In San Francisco Bay, the cargo business moved from San Francisco to Oakland. In Seattle, where there was va-

Container cargo staging areas, Port of Seattle
(Port of Seattle photo)

cant land behind the docks and the opportunity to create more storage space with landfills, the business stayed where it always had been.

By its nature, containerization tends to concentrate trade in single ports. Shipping, trucking, and rail lines all must converge, and there must be elaborate inventory systems to keep track of the thousands and thousands of boxes and all the paperwork that accompanies them. Besides, the guiding principle is speed: get the ship in and out of port and on its way as quickly as possible. A shipping firm doesn't send its vessels ambling down the coast to call at two or three other ports along the way.

When Seattle got the container trade, therefore, its preeminence among Puget Sound ports increased. It was the only port not still tied largely to forest products, and while its share of the Sound's total export tonnage was dropping, its share of the export value was growing by leaps and bounds. In 1967, Seattle shipped 18.8 percent of the export tonnage handled by all Washington ports and 36.6 percent of the value. In 1977, the Port handled only 16.4 percent of the weight but 57.7 percent of the value. Forest products were still a valuable export item, but increasingly, the more a community relied on log exports, the more it seemed a small-time port.

Right: Lauren Donaldson displays a "super trout" (UW, Sneddon photo). Below: At Manchester in the 1970s, the National Marine Fisheries Service launched experiments for raising salmon in saltwater pens (NMFS photo).

the tribes got half the fish

The regional self-image continued to be that of a place in which people cut trees and caught fish for a living. In the case of commercial salmon fishing, the image had less and less to do with reality. Although fishing was still important to some individual communities, its contribution to the regional economy diminished. People still considered fishing important, though, so politically, it still was.

The salient fact about salmon fishing in the 1960s continued to be that more and more fishermen were competing for fewer and fewer fish. The pressure of overfishing wasn't the salmon's only problem. Industrial wastes, municipal sewage, logging practices that destroyed spawning streams, hydroelectric dams that cut off whole river systems had all taken a toll of the native salmon populations. Hatcheries had taken up some of the slack—with genetic consequences that were and are uncertain—but not all. The recommendations made by the University of Washington group in 1963 were never forgotten, but neither were they heeded. Fishermen who used different kinds of gear continued to joust with each other for advantage, but collectively, they never tried seriously to solve their common problems.

The many fishermen who made annual trips to Alaska found it convenient to blame the Japanese who took some Alaskan salmon in the mid-Pacific for the decline of the runs. In Puget Sound, they grumbled about moonlighting school teachers who took a share of the catch for supplemental income, about sport boats, and about each other. Initiative 77's passage in 1934 had closed the southern portion of the Sound to purse seiners. In 1972, the state legislature amended the law to allow purse seining in the lower Sound. The seiners had, of course, lobbied for the change, but disgruntled gillnetters complained that they had bought it outright. Gillnetters said the same thing when the state abolished the regular gillnetting season in Bellingham Bay and decided to open the Bay to all types of fishing gear at times to be determined by the state director of fisheries. Purse seiners countered that the gillnetters were simply selfish. "They say we're taking 'their' fish," one complained at the time. " 'Their' fish!"

By the early 1970s, some commercial fishermen felt threatened not only by each other, but also by the process of economic evolution.

Chasing fish around the Sound was basically a form of hunting. In the late 1960s and early 1970s, fishery scientists began to say that it was time to start fish farming. Near Bellingham, the Lummi Indian tribe, aided by federal funds, built dikes around saltwater ponds, which they stocked with oysters. In freshwater ponds, the Lummis raised Donaldson trout, a species developed by Dr. Lauren Donaldson of the University of Washington. Donaldson, an acknowledged authority on salmon but a controversial public figure, frankly considered traditional fishing methods inefficient and referred to himself as a fish farmer.

He and others argued that there was no reason except politics for continuing to harvest fish in the traditional way. Salmon didn't have to go out to sea and return; all a coho really needed, for example, was at least one cubic foot of water with a current of at least one knot per pound of fish. The fish could be raised in pens, and the biggest pen-raising experiment was launched at Manchester, on the eastern shore of the Kitsap Peninsula, under the direction of Dr. Timothy Joyner. Joyner was quite messianic about the possibilities of raising salmon. Traditional fishing was primitive, he argued; this was the wave of the future. "I feel," he said, "that salmon are ready to become the poultry of the sea."

Naturally that kind of talk made net fishermen uneasy. They were glad to hear that pen-raising projects weren't succeeding economically, that feeding fish in pens wasn't as attractive yet as letting them forage for themselves. Still, aquaculture looked very much as though it might be the upcoming thing. If farming salmon really was the next stage of economic evolution, boat fishermen would soon be on their way to extinction. Inevitably, some of those fishermen were worried.

They would soon be a lot more worried by the reversal of a different evolutionary process. The first people to catch salmon or steelhead on Puget Sound had, of course, been the Indians. When white people settled around the Sound, the Indians continued to fish for their own sustenance. It was also Indian fishermen who supplied the first white fish-salting operations. As the number of whites increased, the Indians were forced out of more and more of their old fishing grounds. White-owned fish traps occupied the old Indian fishing grounds. State game wardens kept the Indians from fishing on the rivers. In some tribes it was said years later that men who went down to the old fishing grounds along the rivers were simply shot.

By the mid twentieth century, there were some Indians in the commercial fishery, working alongside the white fishermen, some who fished from the protected grounds of their reservations, and a very few who persisted in fishing the rivers off their reservations whenever they could evade the game wardens employed by the state. The displacement of the Indian fishery by the whites was not generally considered a big issue around Puget Sound. If people bothered thinking of it at all, they did so in the terms expressed by Richard Rathbun, assistant secretary of the Smithsonian Institution, in 1899. He wrote about the way in which white fish traps had preempted the traditional Indian fishing grounds off Point Roberts. "After the completion in 1894 of the continuous line of traps commanding the approaches to the big reef, its value for [Indian] reef-net fishing seems to have been in great part destroyed, and the Indian catches declined so much in consequence as to render the old-time occupation practically unprofitable," Rathbun wrote. "The primitive methods are making way for those of civilization, and the process has not been wholly devoid of certain elements of injustice." The historical injustice was hard to overlook, but it was seen as an inevitable by-product of "making way for . . . civilization."

It is somewhat ironic that the white boat fishermen and sportsmen had found themselves menaced by the same "methods . . . of civilization" and had legally done away with these more advanced methods in 1934. The Indians had never had the votes or the political organization to take that kind of political action. In the mid-1960s, though, a handful of Indian activists took a lesson from the civil rights movement of the time and started fishing more or less openly, getting arrested repeatedly, drawing press coverage, and dramatizing their cause. Press coverage was greatly increased by the presence of sympathetic celebrities, including actor Marlon Brando and comedian Dick Gregory.

The civil rights movement that led to the federal legislation of 1964 was built on "direct action," not only the highly publicized "freedom rides" into the Deep South, but also a widely dispersed series of "sit-ins" at lunch counters and other spots that customarily refused service to blacks. The people who participated in direct-action campaigns for civil rights sometimes knowingly courted arrest and police brutality, and the Indians and their white supporters who "fished in" on Washington rivers did the same. In the course of their frequent arrests, their fishing gear was confiscated and destroyed, and often they were roughed up. The situation was anything but clear-cut. It was complicated by the personality of a central figure in the earliest years of the fish-ins, Robert Satiacum. Satiacum was accused of profiting indecently from the sale of fish caught during the fish-ins, of single-handedly obliterating at least one whole fish run and eventually, by some fellow Indians, of making his buck and then abandoning the struggle. Even Indians less conspicuously profit-oriented than Satiacum had a thoroughly modern notion of subsistence fishing. When one observed that he and his relatives had enjoyed a good life on the Nisqually River before the state began enforcing its laws so aggressively, he was talking not about the days when they had laid plenty of smoked fish aside for the winter, but about the days when net fishing had brought them an annual income of ten thousand pre-Vietnam dollars.

Even if one stuck to the legal issues, the situation was extremely complex. Most Indian tribes had and still have much the same powers of self-government as sovereign nations, and treaties between them and the U.S. government take precedence over state law. The Indians active in the struggle and the lawyers they hired to represent them argued that the treaties signed with the U.S. government in 1854 and 1855—the treaties that gave the United States title to most of the land around the Sound—guaranteed Indians the right to go on fishing in all their old places, regardless of state laws. The state government and white fishermen did not accept that contention. The treaties said that "the right of taking fish at usual and accustomed grounds and stations is further secured to [the] Indians in common with all citizens of the Territory." According to the state, that meant Indians had the same fishing rights as other citizens, period. Regulation of fishing on the rivers was done by the state Department of Game. The game department had no constituency but the sportsmen, who believed strongly that the rivers should be reserved for people with rods and reels. Consequently, the department had no sympathy for the Indians' fishing methods, and some of its employees evidently had no sympathy for the Indians themselves. Charges of racism were made at the drop of a hat in the 1960s, but one can observe, at the very least, that state game wardens weren't known to have beaten white women for illegal fishing—as they did Indian women—with six-celled flashlights.

When a case from the Puyallup River reached the U.S. Supreme Court in 1968, there was hope that the Court would resolve the legal questions, but the Court chose not to. Instead, it said that the state could regulate Indian fishing off the reservations, but only if such regulation was necessary for conservation, and it had not been proven necessary.

That left virtually everyone unhappy, denying the Indians an absolute right to fish and the state an absolute right to regulate their fishing. It also put the focus more squarely than ever on conservation. The state's regulations were justified on the grounds that they were needed to conserve the fish: if Indians were allowed to use their nets on the rivers, the fish stocks would be depleted. The counter argument was that the laws basically divided the fish up among the competing groups of white fishermen; Indian fishing was a threat to conservation only because all the allowable fish had been divided among whites, and the Indians came at the end of the line.

Some Indians were particularly galled by the Supreme Court's words. The tribes would never get a fair shake from the Court, one complained, because "the Supreme Court is full of conservationists. When most salmon come into the river, they've finished eating. But the steelhead is still hungry as hell. He eats salmon. He eats salmon eggs. And *this* is the fish they want to *protect* in the name of conservation."

The "Battle of the Puyallup River," 1970
(Seattle Magazine, Dolores Varella photo)

The Indians went on fishing. The state kept on arresting them, confiscating their gear, roughing them up. The grand finale, in the summer of 1970, was a charge by some two hundred game wardens and state policemen with tear gas and clubs against Indians on the bank of the Puyallup River in full view of still and movie cameras. The dispute clearly wasn't getting settled. In 1970, to settle it once and for all, the U.S. Attorney for Western Washington, Stan Pitkin, filed a suit in U.S. District Court on behalf of the tribes, many of which later entered the suit on their own, as friends of the court.

While the suit was pending, the state assumed that no judge would convict an Indian arrested for illegal fishing, so it went after the Indians with reduced vigor. If a surplus of fish was expected at a hatchery, it even allowed the Indians to catch some of those fish in the rivers. The sportsmen were outraged. They frankly preferred to see the surplus fish ground up for petfood at the hatcheries—which was actually what became of them—than see them profaned by Indian nets. The sportsmen sent angry delegations to Olympia and campaigned against Daniel J. Evans in the 1972 gubernatorial election.

The State Director of Fisheries, Thor Tollefson—who was for years the source of most state fisheries policy—said that he, personally, welcomed the federal suit. He hoped that, unlike the Supreme Court's 1968 decision, the ruling in *U.S. vs. Washington* would resolve the issue.

Legally it did, but politically it didn't. The case went before an elderly, conservative jurist named George Boldt—the same Boldt who had thrown the oystermen's suit out of court—who had previously made headlines by handing out contempt citations in the trial of the radical "Tacoma 7" and had been rewarded by President Richard Nixon with chairmanship of the federal pay board. Boldt was respected even by attorneys who disagreed with him, and he approached the fishing-rights case, *U.S. vs. Washington*, with great seriousness. His decision covered 254 pages and drew liberally on the history and anthropology of the region. The crux of it was that the tribes got half the fish.

The Indians' share wasn't quite an absolute half. It was half the fish that passed, or normally would pass, by the "usual and accustomed grounds and stations" and could be caught without endangering the runs. If Indians weren't capable of taking half, white fisherman should be allowed to increase their own share. Even with those qualifications, white fishermen and the state government found the decision completely unacceptable. It hit western Washington like the Supreme Court's decision in *Brown vs. Board of Education* hit the Deep South. Although the Ninth U.S. Circuit Court upheld the decision on appeal and the U.S. Supreme Court refused to review it, the opponents remained adamant.

In his 1974 decision in the case of U.S. vs. Washington federal district judge George C. Boldt declared: " 'in common with' means sharing equally the opportunity to take fish at 'usual and accustomed grounds and stations'; therefore, non-treaty fishermen shall have the opportunity to take up to 50% of the harvestable number of fish that may be taken by all fishermen at usual and accustomed grounds and stations and treaty right fishermen shall have the opportunity to take up to the same percentage of harvestable fish . . ." (Seattle Post Intelligencer photo).

Puget Sound gillnetters in protest, Capitol Rotunda, Olympia, October 29, 1976. (Seattle Times, Pete Liddell photo).

Boldt's decision had broadened the conflict. From the rivers, where the sportsmen had been the only white group that felt seriously threatened, he had extended it to the whole Sound and the commercial fishery. More and more fishermen had been chasing fewer and fewer fish for a generation. The conflict among them had been sharpening. The regulatory task for keeping them all in business simultaneously had been growing more complex. Suddenly, they were competing for half as many fish, and a group that had never before been part of the competition had half to itself. Even the trap owners had never been *guaranteed* half the fish. Commercial fishermen were astonished. Some looked for a hidden motive, for some plot that would explain a ruling which on its surface was so blatantly illogical. One explanation was that the major corporations interested in fish farming had put Boldt up to it. The idea was that the corporations wanted a monopoly of the salmon industry. Knowing they couldn't buy the white fishermen off, they decided to turn the fishery over to the Indians, who probably could be bought.

That explanation at least made sense to white fishermen. It made no sense that Indians as Indians should be entitled to more fish than anyone else—"I don't expect anyone to give *me* anything special just because I'm Yugoslavian"—and white fishermen did not really view the treaties as contracts that conferred certain property rights. Nor were they encouraged to do so. The state maintained that special treaty rights didn't exist, and that was the legal advice it gave to fishermen. When a group of angry white fishermen descended on the state capital—after the Ninth U.S. Circuit Court had upheld Boldt—the assistant attorney general in charge of fisheries told them that the decision was "morally reprehensible and unconstitutional."

The fishermen did not want to hear that the decision of the federal court was law and should be obeyed, and by and large, they did not hear it. The state counseled otherwise. The county and state courts ruled otherwise. Most elected politicians were careful to avoid the issue. The only one who suggested it might be a good idea to try living with judicial reality was Congressman Lloyd Meeds, who represented the fishing communities of the upper Sound. Meeds had seemed to have a safe seat, but hostility from fishermen and their sympathizers almost defeated him in the election of 1976.

"Boldt is Nuts" and similar slogans appeared on bumper stickers around the Sound.

Sportsmen were if anything more upset than people who fished commercially. An aide to Meeds pointed out shortly after the Congressman's narrow victory that "the sportsmen feel even more strongly that it's *their* fish." They were absolutely adamant. And since there were some two hundred thousand sportsmen and only about eight thousand commercial fishermen, politicians were quick to suggest that as part of some overall solution to the problem, steelhead, at least, might be exempted from the Boldt decision. The political arithmetic was simple: recreational fishing represented more votes than either treaty rights or commercial fishing did. By some calculations, it contributed more to the economy, too.

Still, the fact remained that steelheaders were fishing for fun—however seriously they took it—and it was the net fishermen, particularly the gillnetters, who felt their livelihoods threatened. Some joined the largely unregulated offshore troll fishery, leaving fewer salmon than ever to be divided among Indian and white net fishermen on the Sound. Some took a clue from the Indians and began "fishing in" themselves, going out on the Sound on nights when everyone but the Indians was forbidden to fish.

White gillnetters "fished in" conspicuously in 1974 and again in the fall of 1976. State patrol boats ran a few of them in. Exactly why the gillnetters were out there was open to question. There was no doubt that they were outraged by Boldt, but some people suspected that for at least a portion of the white fishermen, Boldt was less a reason than an excuse. State records show "illegal fishing for *generations*," an official of the state Department of Fisheries observed. "Each year, prior to Boldt and after Boldt, we've had arrests."

Illegal fishing was clearly profitable. There was one story about a pair of fishermen who rowed out to pick salmon from an illegal set net and piled so many fish into their rowboat that it sank on the way back. Still, the emotions that surrounded the illegal gillnetting weren't strictly mercenary, and the situation was permeated by a tension that hadn't existed in earlier years. Confrontations between fisheries patrol boats and groups of gillnetters became common in 1976. On the night of October 24, 1976, a young Seattle gillnetter was shot in the head by a fisheries patrol officer and paralyzed for life. Earlier in the month, when "fish cops" had tried to arrest a gillnetter fishing near Port Townsend, a couple of dozen other boats had surrounded their patrol boats, circling them and trying to keep them from taking the gillnetter into port. The officers called on a Coast Guard cutter for help. With a .50-caliber machine gun trained on the fishing boats, it escorted the officers and their prisoner into port.

At the end of that season, a number of fishermen started painting boat hulls dark colors and installing big engines, preparing themselves for careers, if necessary, of clandestine fishing. There was widespread fear, at the time, that if the fishing-rights conflict wasn't settled quickly, someone would literally be killed the next time around. Meeds said that "if something isn't done, somebody's going to get killed next year. I think it's just as clear as can be."

Partly because of that fear, Meeds and other members of Washington's congressional delegation pushed for the formation of a federal task force to work out a compromise. The task force was set up on April 8, 1977. From the start, it may have been doomed to fail. The Indians had no particular wish to compromise. They were content with the Boldt decision as it stood and had been upheld by higher courts; they felt, in fact, that they should get more, not less, than Boldt guaranteed them, since they were still taking only a minor share of the Fraser River runs. The white fishermen, particularly the gillnetters, weren't eager to compromise, either; they adamantly opposed the idea that any group had an exclusive right to any percentage of the fish. They wanted the Boldt decision to be thrown out entirely.

Eventually, the task force came up with a suggestion that the Indians stop catching steelhead and agree to take less than fifty percent of the salmon in return for a federally funded enhancement program that would increase the fish population so much that in actual numbers of fish caught, they'd be better off. The gillnetters fought the Boldt decision in court, the Indians rejected the compromise, and the federal government threw up its hands and asked the Supreme Court to review the decision after all. In 1979, the Court did, upholding Boldt in most respects, but leaving some ambiguity about the way in which the catch would actually be divided.

While the legal and not-so-legal maneuvering continued, everyone involved in the conflict talked incessantly of conservation. The days when anyone could talk disparagingly about the Supreme Court being "full of conservationists" was long gone. The white steelhead and commercial fishermen talked about Indians wiping out fish runs. The Indians talked about white net fishermen depleting the runs. Purse seiners said privately that while they hoped the Boldt decision would be thrown out, what really worried them was that the highly profitable, largely unpunished illegal fishing by some of the gillnetters would wipe out the fish for everyone.

The number of commercial fishermen was small, the number of people who really depended on fishing for a living even smaller. The ability of the Boldt decision and the overall fishing-rights conflict to capture thoughts and headlines around the Sound indicated, among other things, how much more significant fishing was psychologically than it was economically. At the height of the tension, one congressional aide suggested that, even for the commercial fishermen, economics were perhaps less important than lifestyle and self-image. Observing that many gillnetters also made money at jobs other than fishing, he said that "being a fisherman is as much 'macho' as it is a way of making a living." Fishermen themselves talked about fishing as a heritage, something they'd like to be able to hand down to their kids. They talked that way whether their families had been fishing for a few generations or a few years.

Obviously, salmon fishing had become an important part of white as well as Indian culture around the Sound. Equally obviously, the Boldt decision had disturbed the delicate balance that had enabled the fishery to continue in its traditional form, compensating for the increased physical efficiency of individual boats by imposing decreased economic efficiency on the fleet as a whole. Right after the Ninth U.S. Circuit Court upheld Boldt, one University of Washington economist who had helped prepare the 1963 report on the salmon fishery suggested that Boldt had simply hastened the inevitable: sooner or later, he said, everyone would have recognized that the number of fishing boats had to be limited. Boldt had made it happen sooner.

Boldt had also undermined the principle, established exactly forty years earlier by Initiative 77, that everyone should have equal access to the fish. The fact that the Indian tribes may have assumed they were getting somewhat more than equal access when they signed the treaties of 1854 and 1855 did not weigh heavily on the minds of many white fishermen. The treaties had not been honored in that respect for more than one hundred years. They did not seem relevant to current conditions. And current conditions were that, even before the Indians got half, there had seemed barely enough fish to go around.

Top: Intalco Aluminum plant near Ferndale. Bottom: Molten aluminum being transferred to a holding furnace where it is kept in a molten state until casting (Intalco photos).

the opening wedge

The struggle over Indian fishing rights was not the only conflict that developed during the 1960s. For the nation as a whole, the decade of the 1960s was filled with conflict, with the flowerings of aggressive political groups and movements. The decade began with the civil rights movement. It ended with the protests against the Vietnam War and the other, less directed turmoil on college campuses—both of which proved short-lived—and the development of a mass environmental movement, which did not.

On Puget Sound, some of what would come to be recognized as "environmental" consciousness had appeared at least as early as the oystermen's first struggles against the pulp industry in the late 1920s. For most of the ensuing years, though—even during the mid- and late 1950s, when the anti-pollution movement broadened its base—concern had focused on the by-products of economic development: on the sulfite wastes emitted by pulp mills, the sewage released by communities in a growing suburbia. During the mid- and late 1960s, concern began to focus on development itself.

The 1950s had seen the oil industry locate, albeit in a relatively small way, along the northern Sound, and the 1960s looked as if they might bring the aluminum industry in force to the same shores. For the Northwest as a whole, the aluminum industry had arrived during World War II, drawn there by the cheap electricity generated at Columbia River dams. Except for a Kaiser aluminum plant on the Tacoma waterfront, the industry had not set up shop on or near Puget Sound. In 1964, though, the Intalco aluminum company set its sights on Cherry Point, north of Bellingham, in Whatcom County. There, it would be easily accessible to ships bringing in Australian bauxite ore. Since it was within the northwestern regional power grid, it would also have access to electricity generated by the Columbia River. At the time, Whatcom County had a fading farm economy toward the coast, with logging in decline farther inland. The county also had a pulp mill and three canneries. Political decision-makers of the county and state welcomed Intalco with open arms. Newspaper editorials were jubilant. The company demanded and got a $2.4 million tax break from the state. The plant produced its first aluminum ingots in 1966.

That same year, another consortium of companies, including two Japanese steel firms, decided to build another aluminum refinery in the Northwest. Courted by the state governments of both Washington and Oregon, the consortium picked Guemes Island, in the Sound just north of Anacortes. It took options to buy some seven hundred and fifty acres of land for which, at the time, there was otherwise a scarcity of willing buyers.

At first, evidently neither the landowners nor anyone else on Guemes knew the identity of the business that had taken options on the land. When people found out that the prospective new occupant of the land was an aluminum refinery, both full-time and summer residents rose up in protest. The refinery would ruin Guemes, they feared, and would be the opening wedge for industrialization of the San Juans. The Save the San Juans Committee was formed, and an anti-aluminum-plant petition was circulated on Guemes itself, gathering 305 signatures. A vote at the Guemes Community Club went 102 to 2 against the aluminum plant.

Not everyone in the area was opposed. Some Guemes property owners steadfastly insisted on their right to sell their land to whomever they chose. Some people on the nearby mainland insisted just as steadfastly that an aluminum plant—any new industrial plant—was just what that area needed. "If that aluminum plant is kept off Guemes Island, the people over there will never be forgiven," the mayor of Anacortes, Jesse Ford, was quoted as saying in the October 1966 issue of *Seattle* magazine. "They'll be hated forever as obstructionists who destroyed the best thing that ever came the way of Anacortes. . . . Anacortes is a working-man's town. Much of our income is seasonal, dependent on fish, lumber and summer crops in the flats. The town can't stand still in an inflated economy, can't live on the low-pay service occupations provided by retirement incomes and tourism. We want to be a real community, not a playground for people who make their money somewhere else. . . . [Anacortes'] people deserve the better things of life. There's a strong possibility of related industries settling right here. [Related industries hadn't congregated around the other aluminum plants in the Northwest, and it's hard to guess what Ford had in mind.] . . . We're due for an industrial boom. What's to conserve?"

For better or worse, Ford's was the old mentality, the any-community-on-the-Sound-can-become-an-industrial-center thinking that had inspired political and business leaders in Puget Sound communities for more than a century. In most of those communities, it had been growing more and more unrealistic ever since World War I. It was also starting to become less fashionable, and by the mid-1960s, one could muster plausible economic arguments against it. The same *Seattle* article quoted the vice-chairman of the Save the San Juans Committee, a Seat-

The Northwest Aluminum Company's announced plans to
build a plant on Guemes Island were abandoned following
the ensuing public controversy (Denman photo).

tle attorney named Howard Tuttle, as saying that "we don't need industry. Nationwide, the American people have invested $58 billion in
retirement funds, so the value of residential-recreational property can't
help but increase—so long as that property is protected for its prime
purpose. As industrial growth proceeds in the state, the islands grow
more important for . . . use as undeveloped retreats." Whether economics provided a reason or a rationale for opposition to the aluminum
plant was uncertain at best. What was certain was that people valued
Guemes and the San Juans for what they were, not for what they could
become. The anti-aluminum forces, aided by the legal work of Seattle
attorney Irving Clark, carried the day. The Northwest Aluminum Company abandoned its plans for Guemes Island and began looking for a
plant site outside Washington State.

It was probably the first time that a major industrial facility had
been driven away from the shores of the Sound, the first time that a
group of people isolated economically by the Sound had insisted
strongly on their isolation. Its importance shouldn't be exaggerated.
There wasn't at the time, and there never developed, a clear consensus
that all economic development should be kept from the Sound, and
there never was unanimity among the entire population of any isolated
place that the isolation should continue. When ARCO decided, three
years later, to build an oil refinery at Cherry Point, there was no storm
of protest. Still, the Guemes incident could be considered a watershed.

The Santa Barbara oil spill at the beginning of 1969 was another
watershed. After Santa Barbara, with its images of fouled beaches and
dying seabirds, "environment" was a national issue. It did not become
an issue out of the blue, of course. "Even as early as 1968," Newsweek
observed in January 1970, "environment was beginning to gain on Vietnam in total lineage in the Congressional Record." In Washington State,
1968 saw the formation of the Washington Environmental Council. The
prime mover behind formation of the Council, and the group's first
president, was Thomas Wimmer. Wimmer felt that the old sportsmen's
groups were too narrowly focused on hunting and fishing and that the
newer environmental groups lacked a broad base of popular support;
he wanted to get both kinds of groups together in one umbrella organization to deal with those issues on which they could all agree. The
WEC was the result. The Northwest as a whole soon became noted for
its profound "environmental consciousness." In Oregon, the environmental movement grew basically out of a concern for the forests. In
Washington, it grew largely out of a concern for the water. Wimmer
himself had become politically active as a member of the Steelhead
Trout Club and had been active in water pollution fights of the 1950s.
During the Washington Environmental Council's first three years of
existence, one of the group's main lobbying goals was state legislation
to protect shorelines.

Within a year after Santa Barbara, U.S. Senator Henry M. Jackson of Everett introduced the National Environmental Policy Act. The Act was signed into law on New Year's Day, 1970, and was followed the next year by a State Environmental Policy Act, patterned closely on it, passed by the Washington State legislature. Both laws required environmental impact statements for any "major governmental actions"—a requirement that opened the door to most of the protracted environmental legal battles of the 1970s. It was true that neither Jackson, who introduced NEPA, nor his staff member, William Van Ness, who drafted it, had any idea that it would be used as it was. It was also true that the state legislators had little idea of what they were passing; Martin Durkan, who had gubernatorial ambitions, introduced the bill as a favor to the environmentalists, and it seemed so innocuously right-thinking that it passed with little furor. Still, the passage of the state and national legislation created an atmosphere of official concern and led soon enough to the significant, highly publicized court cases over the adequacy of impact statements.

In August of the pivotal year, 1970, the Washington Environmental Council announced that, after three unsuccessful lobbying efforts at the state legislature, it was launching an initiative campaign for a law to protect the state's shorelines. The campaign was to be run by Thomas Wimmer, by then the group's ex-president. "We are appalled by what is being done on the shorelines," said the president at the time, Jack Robertson. "The last three legislatures tried to come to grips with it but the special interests wouldn't let them come up with anything meaningful."

The WEC launched its campaign in the middle of the aerospace recession. Nineteen seventy-one began with unemployment in Washington State at twelve percent. Later in the year, the figure was fifteen percent. One might have expected to find a desire for any jobs at any price. That desire existed in some quarters, but it was not general. The WEC collected enough signatures to put its initiative on the ballot in the 1972 general election. The 1971 state legislature quickly passed a similar bill which differed from the WEC's largely in that it gave much greater discretion to county and city governments. Like the WEC's, it required a permit for any significant development on the state's shorelines.

Some ten months before the election of 1972, in January, the history of those shorelines reached another turning point: Weyerhaeuser announced that its old sulfite pulp mill at Everett, one of the most notorious polluters of Puget Sound ever since its opening in 1936, was going to close. It was going to close, *The Seattle Times* reported in a front-page article, "because it is not economically feasible to construct pollution control systems required by the state." In 1969, the state had told Weyerhaeuser to choose a method of reducing its discharge of sulfite liquor by the end of May 1972. In the intervening time, the newly formed federal Environmental Protection Agency had also gotten into the act. The company said the age of the mill made the cost of pollution control unacceptable; besides, even if the company met state standards, the EPA might press it to do more. The director of the state Department of Ecology, John Biggs, said that if the federal government weren't involved, he'd seek some solution other than closing the plant.

The next day, the president of Everett Trust and Savings was quoted as saying, "Unless the ecologists—and I'm one of them—become more realistic, and adopt a more accommodating attitude, we are going to see a long depression."

On January 11, 1972 though, while the story of Weyerhaeuser's forced closure occupied page one of the Times, page fifteen of the fourth section reported that Scott was also going to close one of its two Everett mills "because of a growing surplus of pulp in the world market." The company's general manager observed that "The pulp market just hasn't turned around as we had hoped, and we are now obliged to reduce our production to bring inventories into proper balance."

The next day, the Times reported that the Simpson-Lee Paper Company plant in Everett was closing, too. "The Simpson Lee plant in Everett was built in the 1930s," the paper observed. "The company has purchased a five-year-old plant in Anderson, California, which produces the same kind of pulp." The company's Everett plant would have closed even if there hadn't been pressure to clean up the water.

The impression created—and it wasn't totally inaccurate—was that the heavy hand of anti-pollution laws had finally fallen on the pulp mills of Everett. What the federal EPA found true around the nation, however, was that antiquated mills that would have closed within a couple of years for strictly economic reasons closed a bit sooner and blamed it on the anti-pollution laws.

Weyerhaeuser, for its part, soon built a mill in Everett that employed a "thermo-mechanical" pulping process and didn't spew out any chemical wastes. (The process was roughly forty years old but didn't come into widespread use until the environmentally conscious 1970s.)

The lesson, for many people, was that one could have pulp without pollution—although the pulp produced was not so strong, not so white and therefore not so useful as that produced by chemical means.

For the nation as a whole, water pollution was an important issue in 1972. That fall, right before President Richard M. Nixon won reelection by a landslide over George McGovern, Congress overrode his veto of a $24.7-billion water-pollution-control bill.

In Washington State, Nixon and McGovern shared the November ballot with the Shorelines Management Act. Voters had to decide first whether they wanted any shorelines act at all, and then, if they did, whether they preferred the Washington Environmental Council's Initiative 43 or the state legislature's 43B. The basic idea of a shorelines management act won by about ten percent. The legislature's version, which left more up to the cities and counties, received roughly twice the votes of the WEC's version, which would have put shoreline control firmly in the hands of the state. Even the decentralized form of the Act gave the state a law that would make further industrialization, or even intense residential development, of the shorelines very difficult. Local governments were to develop master programs for the shorelines within their jurisdictions and, using state guidelines, to develop permit systems for "substantial" development along those shorelines.

By that time, the only "substantial development" that seemed likely to occur on any but the eastern shoreline of the Sound was the construction of vacation and retirement homes. Certainly, most of the Sound's western shoreline had no other prospects. The old mill and brickyard towns there had been crumbling for decades. The Bremerton navy yard remained the main employer. The only major new employer was another military installation, the Trident submarine base, built on the eastern shores of Hood Canal. The Navy claimed that for technical reasons—it wanted deep, sheltered water in 1973 for much the same reasons Pope and Talbot had wanted it in 1853—Bangor was the only suitable site on the entire Pacific coast for the high-speed, 535-foot-long, missile submarines. In the six years after 1973, when Bangor was chosen, the population of Kitsap County increased by thirty-two thousand people or roughly thirty percent, a third of which was attributed to the Trident project. As a major military undertaking, the Trident base could, of course, be located without much regard for economics. It was placed on Hood Canal for no economic reason except, perhaps, the alleged desire of Senator Henry Jackson to bring jobs to his constituents.

The days when the Sound was looked on as a highway that could bring industrial development to Port Gamble or Port Townsend or Bainbridge or Vashon were long gone. Even the idea of bridging the Sound to open the islands and the Olympic Peninsula to development had expired with the boom economy and low interest rates of the 1960s.

Not only was bridge-building prohibitively expensive, but also there was no longer any consensus that the isolation of island and peninsula communities was a bad thing. In fact, the people of at least one island fought successfully to protect themselves against faster travel to and from the mainland.

The cause of their anxiety and the target of their wrath was a jet-powered hydrofoil that the Boeing Company had developed during the early 1970s. Originally, Boeing's work on the hydrofoil had impressed virtually everyone as a nice idea: an aerospace company on the shore of an inland sea develops a space-age vehicle that can travel on water. Unfortunately for Boeing, the hydrofoils turned out to be too expensive for the economy of the mid-1970s; they were also plagued—inevitably—with a series of technical problems, and not many were sold. Boeing was still predicting in mid-1977 that two hundred hydrofoils would be in service by the mid-1980s, but so far, it had sold only nine. Understandably, the company was eager to make sales.

As Boeing was developing and trying to market its hydrofoil, the state ferry system was facing a need, or a perceived need, to buy new boats. Traffic was increasing, some of the ferries were fifty years old, and the state was going to have to get new ones. The trouble was, new boats would be expensive, and the state operated its ferry system at a loss. Paying for the construction of new ferries was not an attractive prospect. There seemed to be an out. If the state bought a hydrofoil instead of a conventional ferry, the federal Urban and Mass Transportation Administration might pay eighty percent of the cost. In 1973 and 1977, Boeing lobbied through the state legislature bills that authorized the state to pay its twenty percent share of the cost of two new hydrofoils.

The plan was to operate the two foils morning and night for commuter runs to and from Seattle. That would take some pressure off the regular boats and would enable the foils to qualify as "mass transit." It would also lose money. Taking people back and forth across the Sound wasn't likely to be a paying proposition—not without charging rates that would make old Captain Peabody look like Santa Claus. To make money, the foils would be used at mid-day to take tourists from Seattle to the San Juans or Victoria.

The state was evidently all ready to go, but first it had to get "public input" from the communities that the foils would serve. The first community it chose was Vashon, which was scheduled to be one of the hydrofoils' ports of call. Vashon had been desperately eager for ferry service to downtown Seattle at the time of World War I, had come to rely on that service, had fought to retain it at the end of World War II, had subsequently lobbied for a bridge. But things had changed on the island. More and more of the people who lived there valued their isolation. A series of community meetings had made it clear that virtually everyone wanted the island to stay just as it was. Better, faster connections with downtown Seattle might force changes. A consulting engineer had suggested, in fact, that hydrofoil service would "stimulate the suburbanization of Vashon Island." That was not a popular idea.

Boeing hydrofoils (Boeing photos)

When a five-man team from the ferry system went to Vashon, it found the meeting room filled with people, every chair taken, all the space in the aisles taken, people standing behind the chairs, people standing in the open doorway, people standing outside the doors. The crowd was overwhelmingly hostile. Taken aback, a representative of the ferry system, Kern Jacobson, told his audience that "if Vashon Island doesn't want the service, they're not going to get it." The people at the meeting didn't want it. Some asked for a vote. Jacobson tried to discourage a vote. Finally a man in the crowd stood up and said, "Well, I'm standing against it. Does anybody want to join me?" Most of the crowd stood. Later, when questionnaires distributed at the door were counted, it turned out that 110 out of 120 people present had voted against the hydrofoil. A Vashon-to-Seattle link had been a vital part of the whole hydrofoil plan. "Consequently," Jacobson later explained, at least for the time being, "the whole plan came crashing down."

The lesson was clear: on Vashon, as elsewhere, a lot of people now welcomed the Sound as a protective barrier, a kind of natural moat.

Oil tanker moored at one of the March Point piers near Anacortes (Washington Sea Grant).

clear for a hundred fathoms down

The environmental movement of the late 1960s and the 1970s both created and drew energy from a set of symbols. The real world was not ignored, but certain portions of the real world were perceived as larger—or purer or more sinister—than life. One such portion of the world—the source of the irresistibly symbolic dark stain that could spread across water, beaches, the Alaskan tundra—was the oil industry. Oil development soon became a symbol on Puget Sound—and not only a symbol: all the time the hydrofoil was being proposed, the Shoreline Management Act was being passed, the old pulp mills at Everett were shutting down, the conflict over salmon was intensifying, it seemed possible—and for much of that time, it seemed likely—that a major oil port would be built on the upper Sound. Supertankers would bring up to two million barrels of oil per day in from Alaska. A pipeline would carry it to markets in the Midwest. People who were inclined to worry even vaguely about such things feared a major oil spill in the enclosed waters of the Sound. They thought that a supertanker might collide with one of the tugs, freighters, fishing boats, or pleasure craft that constantly crisscrossed the water. They thought one of the huge, hard-to-maneuver, relatively fragile ships might run aground on a rocky island or submerged reef. Rosario Strait, through which the tankers would have to pass on their way to any likely terminal site on the upper Sound, was narrow and treacherous. Human error was always possible.

Even a large oil spill might cause no more long-term damage than the pulp mills, might pose less of a threat to salmon and steelhead than the haphazard logging practices that routinely destroyed spawning streams, but it was perceived differently. If a spill happened, it would happen without warning. No one knew exactly how much damage a spill might do; depending on the circumstances, the impact might be negligible but it might be cataclysmic. Moreover, unlike the pulp mills, which had been established forty-odd years ago, or the logging practices, which were even older, a major oil spill still seemed preventable.

By the early 1970s, the possibility of such a spill had overshadowed pulp mill pollution as an environmental concern. The mills neither cleaned up nor closed down immediately; the pulp companies, the federal government, and the state—which took the mills' side against the federal government—spent many additional years in court arguing over cleanup goals and dates. But the mills were no longer the center of attention. Nor were the municipalities that continued to discharge sewage into the Sound, nor the modern industries that were pouring pollutants into the marine environment, nor the logging companies that were still damaging salmon-spawning streams. The big issue was oil.

The issue of supertankers on Puget Sound stemmed from construction of the Trans Alaska Pipeline, which itself inspired one of the fiercest and most symbolic environmental conflicts of all time. In 1968, the Atlantic Richfield (later ARCO) and Humble Oil companies announced they had discovered a major oil field under Alaska's North Slope. There was a lot of oil but it was a long way from refineries or markets. The oil companies soon decided to get it out of the Arctic by pumping it through a 780-mile pipeline to Valdez, a small, ice-free port in Southeast Alaska. The building of the pipeline would be the largest private construction project in history. Much of it would take place in the middle of the last real wilderness in the United States. The conflicts—between pipeline and wilderness, between preservation of the Alaska tundra and caribou and preservation of a petroleum-based economy— were classic. By the end of 1969, the oil companies had ordered eight hundred miles of forty-eight-inch steel pipe from Japan; one hundred miles of the pipe were already stacked at Valdez, and the commitment to a pipeline was irrevocable.

It was also made without a clear sense of where the oil would go next. Valdez was almost as remote from refineries and markets as the North Slope. The two million barrels of oil a day that were expected to flow through the pipeline obviously would have to be taken someplace else. The oil would have to travel in big tankers. No one knew for certain where the tankers would go.

The closest harbors in the "lower 48" states lay in Puget Sound. In 1969, ARCO applied for the state and federal permits necessary to build a highly automated refinery at Cherry Point. The refinery would not be large enough to handle all or even most of the oil from the North Slope, though, and it was still far from markets in the Midwest or East, so two questions remained: Where would the rest of the oil enter the "lower 48" states? And, how would it be transported to the Midwest and East?

The oil might all go by tanker to a port in Puget Sound, then be pumped through a pipeline to the Midwest. In December 1969, ARCO's executive vice-president, Louis Ream, told six hundred northwestern businessmen that a pipeline from Puget Sound was one of the most likely ways, and perhaps the most likely way, of getting the oil to eastward markets.

Some people welcomed that prospect—it conjured up images of a second Alaskan gold rush, with the Puget Sound area booming once again—but others didn't. Nineteen sixty-nine had begun with the Santa Barbara oil spill, and images of fouled beaches and oil-soaked seabirds were fresh in people's minds. The breaking up of the tanker *Torrey Canyon*, which fouled the beaches of Dover and Cornwall, had occurred only two years before. Now, the Trans Alaska Pipeline had become a focus of environmental debate. If crude oil from the North Slope was a menace to tundra and caribou, what might it do to the beaches and sealife of Puget Sound? By early 1970, a hand-lettered sign over the doorway to the Seattle office of the Sierra Club proclaimed "If the Puget Sound—Chicago oil pipeline is built, we will have to start measuring our tides with a dipstick. Anacortes will join Cornwall, Dover, and Santa Barbara in the ranks of the great ecological disasters of our time. Help stop this betrayal of our earth."

Not even oil-company executives ever advocated taking major risks with the Sound, but people disagreed about the degree of risk that large tankers would create and about the best ways of reducing or avoiding that risk. Relatively small tankers had been carrying oil into Puget Sound for years. (Shortly after Mobil built its refinery at Ferndale, in 1954, the refinery's manager sent a letter to Mobil customers proclaiming that "we are . . . equipped . . . to handle the largest tankers in the world." No one batted an eye.) The oil companies and some state officials believed that by increasing the sizes and numbers of tankers entering the Sound, they would not materially increase the risk of a serious spill. Others were less sanguine. The 1971 state legislature passed a law imposing unlimited liability for oil-spill damage on whoever was responsible. Since federal law limited oil-spill liability to $14 million, the Washington law was an expression of more-than-average concern.

The next year, an aerospace engineer named Robert Lynette organized a citizen's group called the Coalition Against Oil Pollution to keep large tankers out of Puget Sound, or at least make them safer. The coalition never became a mass movement—one longtime member observed in the late 1970s that while the group had created an illusion of numbers, "it was all run out of Bob Lynette's basement"—but it did provide a focus, a voice, and a lobbyist for broadly based public ideas and fears.

The fears were real, but the amount of damage a large oil spill would do remained a matter of conjecture. A study made by Texas Instruments of a small 1971 diesel oil spill at Anacortes concluded that the short-term impact had been severe. No long-term studies had been made in the Sound, though, and few had been made anywhere else. (Not that long-term studies were easy to make. If it was hard to draw casual connections between pulp-mill pollution and the decline of oyster populations, it was all but impossible to show, in the field, the cumulative effects of an oil spill not massive enough to kill large numbers of fish immediately. Petroleum contains hundreds of chemical compounds, many of which are altered by exposure to air, light, or microorganisms. It is hard enough just to trace the original compounds through a food chain, much less to prove that any one of them is directly responsible for, say, an increased number of genetic defects or decreased resistance to disease within a given population of fish.) The absence of evidence did not prevent either public officials or interested citizens from holding strong opinions. "You don't need studies to know what effect an oil spill would have in Puget Sound," former Senator Warren Magnuson told a 1971 press conference at the Bellingham Hotel—"Why, it would be disastrous!"

Like thousands of other people, Magnuson clearly had an emotional attachment to the Sound, which he has often referred to as "the most pristine estuary in the world." But he was not concerned with preserving it only for aesthetic or cultural reasons. He believed strongly in the economic value of a clean Sound. Then, and as the 1970s progressed, he was eager to preserve the established fishing and recreation industries and even more eager to preserve the Sound's potential for aquaculture.

In most of the United States, it was hard to escape a conflict between environmentalism and economics: between, say, keeping water clean and keeping people employed. On Puget Sound, the distinction was no longer clear. Clean water meant jobs and income—fewer jobs, perhaps, than people interested in opposing supertankers sometimes claimed, but even the beleaguered fishing industry supported more jobs than a port for the largest conceivable supertankers would provide. The value in hard cash of visitors from other parts of the state and nation was legitimately up in the tens of millions of dollars by the early 1970s, and between 1972 and 1977 it probably doubled. If one took the prospect of aquaculture seriously—and a National Marine Fisheries Service scientist estimated in 1974 that if oysters were raised in even half the area of Puget Sound that was suitable for raising them, the annual harvest could be six billion pounds—the economic value of clean water increased exponentially. Refinery workers' unions and major oil companies might disagree, but one could argue plausibly that big tankers should be kept out of the Sound for the long-term good of the economy.

At first, the only perceived reason for bringing big tankers in was that Alaskan oil would have to go *somewhere*. As the decade progressed, other politically more urgent reasons developed. In 1970 Washington and the "Northern Tier" states of the Midwest got most of their oil by pipeline from Canada. In 1974, the Canadians announced that the flow of oil would stop in 1983. In 1975, they moved the cutoff date up to 1981. By that date, all of Washington's oil would presumably

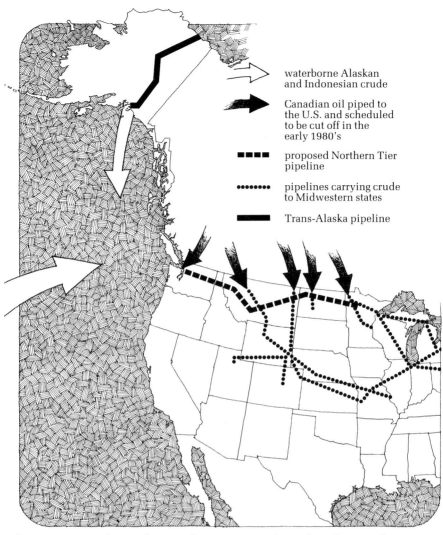

waterborne Alaskan
and Indonesian crude

Canadian oil piped to
the U.S. and scheduled
to be cut off in the
early 1980's

proposed Northern Tier
pipeline

pipelines carrying crude
to Midwestern states

Trans-Alaska pipeline

have to arrive by tanker, and—more significantly—the Northern Tier
would have to get its oil by pipeline from some port on the West Coast.

By that time it was clear that, despite pressure from Magnuson and
others, the Coast Guard didn't want to impose construction standards
on American tankers that were not imposed on the tankers of other nations. People who worried about the safety of supertankers in Puget
Sound wanted the vessels to be equipped with double bottoms, to put
an extra layer of steel between the oil and the water, twin screws, to
make the vessel more maneuverable, and other expensive features. Because of the Jones Act, it would have been feasible to impose those
standards on all the new tankers that would carry oil south from
Alaska. There was no guarantee that the Northern Tier would be supplied with Alaskan oil, though, and in fact, the largest tankers carrying
oil to Cherry Point had been loaded in Indonesia.

When it became clear that the Coast Guard had neither the will nor, in some cases, the authority to force extra safety features on tankers that might enter Puget Sound, the 1975 session of the state legislature took matters into its own hands—after a very determined lobbying effort— and passed what was known as the "tanker" or "tug escort" law, which placed extremely strict limits on the operation of supertankers in Puget Sound. No tanker of more than 125,000 deadweight tons was permitted to enter the Sound. Any tanker of more than 50,000 deadweight tons either had to be equipped with a double bottom, twin screws, and colli- sion-avoidance radar, or be accompanied by a tug at all times.

Passing that law was a big step for any state legislature to take. No other state had attempted anything comparable. Still, what the anti-oil forces had hoped for all along was to keep big tankers entirely out of Puget Sound. If an oil terminal were located at or west of Port Angeles, tankers wouldn't have to pass through Rosario Strait or other extremely congested areas; if a spill did occur there, the oil would more likely be dispersed and carried out to sea. In 1973, 1974, and 1975, bills were introduced in the state legislature at the request of Governor Evans that would have prevented the location of a terminal east of Port Angeles. None of the bills passed. The oil companies that already operated small refineries on the upper Sound didn't want the extra expense of piping oil in from Port Angeles, and none wanted to rely on a terminal or pipe- line over which it did not exercise direct control.

In 1975, when Canada announced that it would cut off the Northern Tier's oil supply within six years, private industry—not the oil industry on Puget Sound—added impetus to the movement for an oil port outside the inner Sound. The Northern Tier Pipeline Company proposed building a terminal at Port Angeles and piping oil east from there to the Northern Tier states. The oil companies operating small re- fineries near Bellingham and Anacortes could, if they wished, tie into the Northern Tier line with a north-south pipe running along the east- ern shore of the Sound.

In 1976, Northern Tier formally applied for a permit to build such a terminal at Ediz Hook, near Port Angeles. The oil companies and the refinery-workers' union opposed the idea. Many Port Angeles citizens opposed it, too. The Evans administration did not grant a permit.

Under the terms of the federal Coastal Zone Management Act, though, Washington was drawing up legislation that was to make it the first state in the country with a federally approved plan for its coastal zone. The anti-tanker lobby slipped in language that explicitly forbade an oil port on the inner Sound. The oil lobby, apparently caught nap- ping, did not object. Evans signed the bill. When 1976 ended, an inner- Sound oil port was forbidden by law.

But the Evans administration was over. The incoming governor, Dixy Lee Ray, had made it clear that she considered the opposition to supertankers sheer nonsense. Alaskan oil would begin flowing through the Trans Alaska Pipeline in 1977, and there was still no port anywhere on the West Coast with facilities for piping it to the Midwest. In addition, ARCO, which had already brought tankers of more than 125,000 deadweight tons to its Cherry Point refinery, had gone to court to challenge the constitutionality of the tug-escort law. In 1976, a special three-judge federal panel ruled against the state. The next year, the U.S. Supreme Court upheld that ruling.

Most state legislators were not following these legal and political developments with bated breath. Most did not even really know what was going on. Still, protection of the Sound had become something of a motherhood issue, there was no love lost between the legislature and Governor Ray, and in early 1977, the legislators passed a law that would have confirmed the ban on supertankers in the inner Sound. Ray vetoed it.

That was the final straw. Members of Washington's congressional delegation felt that something had to be done, and done quickly. First-term Representative Norm Dicks, Magnuson's former administrative assistant, attached an amendment to an appropriations bill that would have prevented the Army Corps of Engineers from granting permits for the construction of oil-terminal piers. Dicks's amendment, indirect though it was, looked to most observers like the best bet for stopping tankers through federal legislation. But Magnuson had his own legislation ready. He was just waiting for the right time to introduce it.

The Senate had just returned from lunch on October 4, 1977, when Magnuson rose to make an unexpected speech. At first glance, the speech was strictly routine. The Senate had passed a bill to increase appropriations for the Marine Mammal Protection Act. The House had amended the bill. Now Magnuson, as chairman of the Senate Commerce Committee, suggested that the Senate accept the amendment. So far, it was not only routine; it was downright boring. But there was more.

Magnuson also wanted the Senate to accept an amendment of his own. "The second amendment is extremely important to me and to the State of Washington," he said. "The State of Washington has been experiencing a heated public debate on the location of expanded oil terminal facilities in the State's coastal zone. While I would have preferred a unanimous decision by State leaders settling this controversy, unfortunately, this has not happened. Instead of allowing this controversy to continue, I and my colleagues from the State have decided to confirm, as a matter of federal law, that increased tanker traffic in Puget Sound is simply bad policy and should not be allowed."

Right: Former Senator Warren G. Magnuson
Below: Magnuson presiding over a late
night session of the Senate Appropriations
Committee (Blindheim photos)

Despite Magnuson's statement that "I and my colleagues from the State" had reached a decision, most of his colleagues in Congress, to say nothing of state officials and even his own political allies back home, had no idea of what he was going to do. He evidently wanted it that way. The legislation would have to come as a surprise and be pushed through quickly—if possible, by unanimous voice votes in both houses—so that the opposition wouldn't have a chance to gather strength.

The Senate had not known what to expect. Senator Henry Jackson evidently learned about the legislation when he walked in during Magnuson's speech. Jackson, much closer than Magnuson to Dixy Lee Ray and more preoccupied with the problems of national energy supply, was reportedly outraged. But he did not oppose the amendment. No one else did, either, and it passed without objection.

The next step was to get it through the House of Representatives. There, too, Magnuson had played his cards very close to his vest. In the House, the amendment fell into the bailiwick of the Committee on Merchant Marine and Fisheries. Magnuson had confided in the two Washington members of the Committee, Don Bonker, a Democrat, and Joel Pritchard, a Republican. He had also confided in the committee's chairman, John M. Murphy, a Democrat from New York.

Murphy introduced the amendments in the House that same afternoon. This time, there was a hitch. John Baumann, a Maryland conservative to whom the House Republicans had given the task of keeping an eye on all proposed legislation, spotted the Magnuson proposal and objected. The House had just passed a bill that would have made it illegal to use federal funds for abortions. The Senate had refused to pass it. The abortion issue was important to Baumann, and he wanted to make passage of the anti-tanker amendment contingent on Magnuson's support for the abortion bill.

Murphy didn't press the issue—a unanimous vote was still the object—and the bill went nowhere that afternoon.

Magnuson let Baumann know that he absolutely refused to link his tanker amendment to the abortion issue. In case there was a fight on the House floor, he lined up the support of House Speaker Thomas P. O'Neill, but he still preferred to have the legislation passed without objection. To win Baumann over, he called on the only conservative member of the Washington delegation, first-term Congressman Jack Cunningham. Cunningham and Magnuson were miles apart ideologically, but they had similar feelings about tankers in the inner Sound. It was Cunningham who had drafted and introduced the tug escort law in the 1975 state legislature. Cunningham went to see Baumann, and he succeeded.

When Murphy reintroduced the amendment as the first order of business the next day, Baumann withdrew his objection. "The only reason I am withdrawing my objection today," he said, "is because I have discussed the pending matter with [Cunningham]. He has explained to me that he was the author of a similar state law and this is very important to him and to the State of Washington . . . his arguments were most persuasive."

The amendment sailed through on a voice vote.

The final step was getting it signed by President Carter. There was opposition, but the Magnuson forces called on all their allies on the White House staff, Magnuson told Carter personally that the bill was extremely important to him, and the President signed.

That was that. The oil issue wasn't entirely moot—there would continue to be debates over the siting of terminals at Port Angeles and at Kitimat, British Columbia, and, of course, what Congress had done it could undo—but for the time being, an oil port in the inner Sound was out of the question. (The Coalition Against Oil Pollution had advocated an oil port at Port Angeles as an alternative to one on the inner Sound, but soon after Magnuson's legislation passed, many other environmentalists were to argue wholeheartedly against the Port Angeles location, too. They grew, if anything, more hostile when discussion turned to a Northern Tier pipeline beneath the Sound, rather than around it.) Governor Ray could call Magnuson's action "dictatorial," but she was faced with a *fait accompli*. And there is no evidence that the citizens of the state shared her objections. Quite the contrary. A private poll taken shortly after Magnuson's victory indicated that eighty-five percent of the adults in Washington approved of what he had done. His office received 483 letters about the anti-oil-port legislation; 412 were favorable, only 71 opposed. "You settled the issue," wrote an elected official from the San Juans, "and God bless you."

The point is not that Magnuson should be regarded as a single-handed savior of the Sound. If, in fact, he had been a lone environmental crusader acting in political isolation, his legislative coup would have been much less significant. (It might also have been impossible.) But, of course, he was nothing of the kind. He had held elected office for more than forty years, was the second most senior member of the U.S. Senate. He had become widely known—in some circles notorious—for looking after the economic welfare of his constituents. People said he had a "gut feeling" for the mood of the electorate that was second to none. That Magnuson, the consummate practical politician, should introduce such legislation was extremely significant.

Industrializing the shoreline of the Sound was no longer a regional aspiration. Economically, the water was still important as a conduit to the outside world. If it no longer enabled the surrounding communities to ship goods cheaply among themselves, it still enabled some—as in the earliest years of white settlement—to sell their largely unprocessed logs in distant ports. Keeping large tankers out certainly wouldn't jeopardize that trade. Nor would it jeopardize the extremely profitable container trade that good harbors and intelligent capital investment had created, or the close commercial relationships with Alaska and the Orient that geography had made all but inevitable.

The water was as deep and sheltered as ever—hence the Trident submarine project—and it still supported a great deal of marine life. Salmon were no longer a staple but a luxury, had declined in number and in some cases disappeared, but salmon were still there and still provided at least partial incomes to more people than an oil port would ever employ. No one could really gauge the Sound's potential for aquaculture; maybe all the speculation about it was simply a form of economic utopianism. But theoretically, at least, there was no reason why aquaculture couldn't work and why it couldn't be immensely profitable. Business economists who looked scornfully on the fish-*catching* industry's claims to economic importance thought that fish *farming* might actually become something big. Recreation and tourism—although the figures usually attached to them were obviously inflated—were clearly already big.

To say that supertankers should be kept out because they might endanger the current fishing, recreation and tourism industries, and might destroy the potential growth of all those industries plus aquaculture was plausible enough. But to some extent, those were economic arguments being advanced to justify non-economic impulses. People liked being able to see the sunlight glinting on the wave crests and to know that the water was clear for a hundred fathoms down. They liked catching salmon in the water, or at least knowing salmon were there; liked seeing pods of killer whales swim through, their shiny black-and-white bodies breaching the surface of the water, puffing like locomotives as they passed. They liked being able to walk beaches of scoured rock and smooth, gray driftwood, knowing in many cases that the Sound kept the pressures of industrial civilization away from those beaches and from the woods and vestigial farmlands behind them. If a twentieth-century economy could be based on that "pristine" water, so much the better. The evidence suggested that it was possible. Certainly, a lot of people were eager to try.

Chronological Table
Bibliographic Notes
Index

Chronological Table

National International	On Puget Sound	Timber industry Pulp/paper industry
1846—Boundary of Oregon Country settled with Great Britain		
1848—Mexican War ends		
1849—California gold rush		**1849**—Pope and Talbot establish lumber firm in California
1850s—Extension of slavery into new territories is major political issue		
1852—Commodore Perry opens trade with Japan		**1853**—W.C. Talbot sails to Puget Sound seeking lumber for San Francisco building boom; establishes sawmill on Hood Canal; by late 1853, sawmills operating at Port Gamble, Port Ludlow, Appletree Cove, Alki, Seattle
1853—Franklin Pierce becomes President	**1853**—Washington territory splits off from Oregon Country	
1854—Crimean War	**1854-55**—U.S. acquires land around Puget Sound through treaties with Indians	
1860—Pony Express established		**1855**—Mill established on Camano Island to cut spars for French and Spanish navies
1861-65—Civil War		
1864—Lincoln signs bill offering land as inducement to build railroad to Puget Sound		
1867—U.S. purchases Alaska from Russia		
	1870s—San Francisco remains major source of capital and is major market for Sound's timber, coal, and salted salmon	**1870s**—San Francisco is major market for Sound's timber
1873—Panic causes scarcity of capital	Most towns are company owned—principally by San Francisco firms; exceptions are Seattle, Port Townsend, Olympia, Tumwater, Steilacoom	
1876—Bandsaw introduced at Centennial Exposition in Philadelphia		
1878—Timber & Stone Act enables citizens to acquire 160 acres of public timber lands at $2.50 per acre		

Commercial/Sport fishing Seafood processing	Waterborne commerce Transportation/Ports	Other industries
	1860s—Hall Brothers ship-yard begins operations on Camano Island	**1860s**—Coal discovered on Puget Sound; mines at Bellingham and east of Seattle; San Francisco is chief marketplace
	1865—Regular waterborne connections established between Seattle and Bainbridge Island	
	1869—Regular waterborne connections between Seattle and Kitsap Peninsula	
1870s—San Francisco is major market for Sound's salted salmon		
1870—Canadians begin commercial canning of Fraser River salmon		
1872—Dogfish oil extraction plant set up on McNeil Island	**1873**—Railroad construction halted due to panic	
1877—First fish cannery on Puget Sound built at Mukilteo	**1875**—Hall Brothers ship-yard moved to Port Blakely	

National International	On Puget Sound	Timber industry Pulp/paper industry
1880—Congressional commission asks for repeal of the Timber & Stone Act because of abuses	**1880s**—End of frontier isolation	**1880s**—Beginning of logging railroads
1882—Edison starts first commercial electric generating plant	**1886**—Knights of Labor begin organizing longshoremen and sailors	Crosscut saw replaces ax as logger's principal tool Bandsaw increases sawmill daily output tenfold
1886—Western movement for silver-backed currency	**1889**—Washington becomes a state	**1883**—William Renton writes that 'the timber contiguous to the Sound is nearly exhausted'
1888—Canada disputes U.S. boundary	**1889**—Commission recommends Bremerton as navy yard site	
1888—Congress authorizes navy yard in Northwest	**1889**—Seattle fire	**1888**—St. Paul and Tacoma Lumber Company established by Minnesota and Wisconsin lumbermen; operations begin in 1889
1890s—Japan developing as naval power	**1890**—Second commission reaffirms selection of Bremerton for navy yard	
1890—Congress appoints second site selection commission for Northwest navy yard	**1892**—Contract awarded to construct naval drydock at 'Port Orchard'	
1891—Shipping Act	**1892**—Confrontation between Seattle longshoremen and merchant vessel *Haitian Republic*	
1892—Prosilver People's Party runs candidate for president	**1892**—Seattle Yacht Club founded; schedules 'national' regatta	
1893-97—Depression	**1897**—*City of Portland* unloads ton of gold in Seattle and sets off Klondike gold rush	
1895—300 automobiles registered in U.S.		**1898**—Frederick Weyerhaeuser, Midwest timber baron, buys into Coast Lumber Company
1898—Spanish-American War	**1898**—Seattle becomes banker and supplier to Alaska resource development firms	
1899-1902—Boer War		**1899**—Weyerhaeuser buys timberlands around Skagit and Sauk Rivers
1901—President William McKinley assassinated	**1900**—Expansion of Bremerton navy yard	**1900**—Weyerhaeuser purchases 900,000 acres of land-grant timberland from Northern Pacific Railroad
1903—Alaskan Boundary Tribunal, London, rules against Canadian claim	**1900s**—Summer homes being built on Kitsap Peninsula and southern Sound islands by city dwellers	**1900-05**—Steam donkey, bandsaw, more capital, expanded markets contribute to increased production of lumber
1903—Wright brothers make first powered flight	**1905**—Industrial Workers of the World founded; primary support is in logging camps	
1906—San Francisco destroyed by earthquake and fire	**1905**—Union locals in Seattle form Central Labor Council	**1906**—Rebuilding San Francisco provides bonanza for Northwest lumber mills
1908—Canada and U.S. establish commission to study/recommend management strategies for Fraser River salmon		

Commercial/Sport fishing Seafood processing	Waterborne commerce Transportation/Ports	Other industries
1880s—Fish traps introduced; erected mostly by canneries	**1880s**—Northern Pacific Railroad completed between St. Paul and Tacoma	
1888—Three Massachusetts schooners open halibut fishery on Strait of Juan de Fuca		**1888**—St. Paul syndicate erects smelter in Tacoma; operations begin in 1889
1900s—Canneries still primarily dependent on fish traps and upon cheap Chinese labor	**1893**—Great Northern Railroad completed to Seattle	
1900—Puget Sound halibut schooners fishing in Alaskan waters		
1903—Iron Chink, an automated machine for heading/gutting salmon installed at Bellingham cannery		
1903—First motorized purse seiner appears off Point No Point		
1909—Canada/U.S. commission recommends regulation of fish traps and commercial fishing boats and limiting fishing to five days during every week of fishing season—Agreement never signed		**1905**—*Inland Flyer* converts from coal to oil—first in Mosquito Fleet to burn oil

The Water Link / Chasan

National International	On Puget Sound	Timber industry Pulp/paper industry
1908—Henry Ford introduces first mass-produced automobile—Model T		1909-10—Economic slump diminishes markets for Puget Sound lumber
	1914-19—War creates markets for Sound lumber, fish, harbors, and shipbuilding sites	1910s—Federal government cuts and processes Olympic Peninsula spruce for aircraft
1914—World War I begins in Europe		1914—Lumber industry strike loses support for I.W.W.
1914—Panama Canal is completed		1915—Weyerhaeuser opens sawmill at Everett
1916—Congress establishes U.S. Shipping Board to regulate merchant marine and promote shipbuilding	1917—Roads completed along Hood Canal; steamer service ends on Canal	
1917—U.S. enters World War I	1919—Seattle general strike lasts eight days to protest end of wartime jobs and wage levels	
1920—Senator Wesley Jones of Washington sponsors bill to finance shipbuilding and to limit cargo carriers between U.S. ports to U.S. ships; Jones Act passed by Congress		1920s—Pulp industry arrives
		1926—Twelve counties around Puget Sound produce 5.79 million board feet of timber
		late 1920s—Mark Reed persuades Zellerbachs of San Francisco to build pulp mill in Shelton to utilize sawmill wastes
1929—Wall Street crash		

166

Chronological Table

Commercial/Sport fishing Seafood processing	Waterborne commerce Transportation/Ports	Other industries
c. 1909—Seiners begin rigging boats with masts and booms to facilitate lifting netfuls of salmon aboard		
1911-19—Peak years for Pacific Northwest salmon pack		
1913—Record year for Fraser River salmon		
1913—Hells Gate rockslide cuts off Fraser River salmon from spawning grounds		
1914—First marine diesel engine appears in commercial fleet	**1914**—Port of Seattle's domestic imports exceed domestic exports	
1916—Most commercial boats are motorized; fishing communities growing up around the Sound. Fresh fish being landed at canneries throughout the Sound	**1914-19**—Foreign trade through Washington Customs District quintuples	**1916**—Boeing begins building aircraft in Seattle
1919—Gasoline motors widespread throughout commercial fleet; Puget Sound seiners begin cruising north to Alaska	**1918**—Puget Sound ports handling more cargo than any U.S. port save New York and more trade with Orient than any other U.S. port	
1920s—During this decade, approximately 1,200 commercial boats are licensed annually; however, fish traps continue to catch most salmon landed	**1920s**—Mark Reed lures Northern Pacific Railroad to Shelton	
1920s—Steelhead fishermen organize to oppose poachers		
1926—State fisheries board appoints Investigation Committee on Pollution Problems		
1928—Steelhead Trout Club formed; launches campaign against poachers		
1929—Legislature declares steelhead a game fish in fresh waters		
1929—Decline of commercial oyster beds in southern Sound causes Olympia Oyster Growers Association to complain over pulp mills		

167

National International	On Puget Sound	Timber industry Pulp/paper industry
1930s—General strike in San Francisco	**1930s**—Depression reaches Puget Sound businesses	**1930s**—Depression causes closure of some mills
	1930s—Communities around Lake Washington begin treating sewage	
1933—Franklin D. Roosevelt inaugurated as President	**1930s**—Labor troubles on Seattle waterfront	
	1934—Seattle dock strike	
		1935—Mill worker strike forces mills to recognize unions
1939—World War II begins in Europe		**1940**—Twelve Puget Sound counties produce 2.96 million board feet of timber
1941—U.S. enters World War II		**1940s**—Weyerhaeuser begins investing in machinery and plants for manufacturing pulp and paper
	1945—Legislature passes bill to establish Pollution Control Commission	
	1948—Arthur Langley elected governor of Washington	
	1950s—Economic doldrums for Sound ports	
1951—Federal report indicates Puget Sound is sixth most polluted area in country		
1957—Russians launch Sputnik into space	**1955**—State Pollution Control Act requires permits for dumping wastes into public waters	
	1958—METRO created to construct and administer regional sewage system	
1960s—Civil rights movement	**1960s**—Washington Environmental Council formed	
1961—Federal Water Pollution Control Act	**1961**—Federal-state conference on water pollution convenes in Olympia	**1961**—Pollution Control Commission sets deadlines for seven mills to clean up wastes

Commercial/Sport fishing Seafood processing	Waterborne commerce Transportation/Ports	Other industries
1930—Of 257 fish trap licenses issued, 172 are controlled by nine operators		
1930—Shelton area oystermen receive out-of-court settlements from pulp mill		
1932—Steelheaders launch successful initiative campaign to establish State Departments of Fisheries and of Game		
1934—Initiative 77 results in ban of fish traps		**1935**—Boeing builds B-17 bomber
1937—U.S. signs treaty with Canada for joint management of Fraser River sockeye		
	1940s—Throughout the war shipbuilding industry booms—total contracts in 1943 exceed total value of all pre-war manufacturing in state	**1940s**—Boeing's work force expands from 4,000 to 45,000
1944—Fish ladder built around Hells Gate rockslide	**1940**—Tacoma Narrows Bridge opens and collapses five months later	
	1948—State supreme court declares purchase of Black Ball system unconstitutional	
1950s—United States calls for reduction of high seas net fishing	**1950s**—Bridges built at Agate Pass and across Hood Canal; new bridge built across Tacoma Narrows	**1950s**—Mobil builds first oil refinery on Puget Sound
1951—Nylon nets begin to replace linen gillnets	**1951**—State buys ferry system	
1955—Power block for hauling seine nets out of water introduced		
1960s—Foreign fleets dominate many U.S. coastal waters	**1960s**—Port of Seattle invests in facilities for handling container cargoes	
1962—University of Washington committee begins economic and management survey of State's salmon fishery		

National International	On Puget Sound	Timber industry Pulp/paper industry
1963—President John F. Kennedy assassinated		
1964—Federal civil rights legislation		
1968—Oil discovered on North Slope of Alaska		
1969—U.S. astronauts land on moon	**1969**—Beginning of aerospace recession	
1969—Oil spill at Santa Barbara	**1970s**—Washington Environmental Council launches shoreline protection initiative; legislature passes similar bill	**1970s**—Weyerhaeuser builds mill in Everett employing thermo-mechanical rather than chemical pulping process; closes mill built in 1936
1970—National Environmental Policy Act becomes law	**1971**—Regional unemployment reaches 15%	
1971—Congress votes down Boeing bid to build supersonic transport (SST) plane	**1971**—State legislature passes State Environmental Policy Act	**1970s**—Japan provides major market for regional log exports—public opposition to exports mounts
1971—Congress overrides Nixon veto of water-pollution-control bill	**1971**—Washington citizens approve legislative version of Shoreline Management Act	
1972—Nixon defeats McGovern		**1972**—Scott and Simpson-Lee pulp mills close in Everett
1973—Arab oil embargo	**1972**—Coalition Against Oil Pollution organized to oppose tankers on Puget Sound	
1974—Canada announces flow of oil through northern pipeline will stop in 1983	**1975**—Legislature passes tug escort law	
1975—Canadians move oil flow deadline to 1981	**1976**—Washington becomes first state with federally approved plan for coastal zone management	
	1976—Tug escort law challenged; federal panel rules against state	
1977—Senator Warren Magnuson sponsors federal legislation banning oil ports on inner Puget Sound	**1977**—U.S. Supreme Court upholds panel ruling preventing state from excluding large tankers on Puget Sound	

Commercial/Sport fishing Seafood processing	Waterborne commerce Transportation/Ports	Other industries
1963—Committee recommends gear reductions, increased license fees, buy-back program		**1964**—Intalco announces Cherry Point as site for aluminum company
1964—U.S. District Judge George Boldt dismisses oyster growers' suit against pulp mill		**1966**—Consortium decides to build aluminum refinery on Guemes Island; plans successfully opposed by citizens
1968—First U.S. Supreme Court decision on Indian fishing rights		**1966**—Boeing sets up 747 plant in Everett
1970s—Lummi Indian tribe builds fish farm near Bellingham; NMFS begins rearing salmon in pens near Manchester	**1970**—Six Japanese shipping lines choose Seattle as northwestern port of entry	**1969**—ARCO builds oil refinery at Cherry Point
1970—Game wardens and Indians battle on banks of Puyallup River		**1969-71**—Boeing lays off half its workers
1970—U.S. Attorney for Western Washington files suit on behalf of tribal fishing interests		**1970s**—Ports begin developing marinas for pleasure craft
1972—Legislature opens southern Sound to commercial seiners		**1970s**—Boeing develops jet-powered hydrofoil
1974—U.S. District Judge George Boldt rules that treaty Indian tribes are due 50% of fish harvests		
1975—Boldt decision upheld by Ninth U.S. Circuit Court		
1976—U.S. Supreme Court refuses to hear appeal of Boldt decision		**1976**—Northern Tier applies for permit to build oil terminal near Port Angeles
1976—'Fish-ins' result in shooting of gillnetter by fisheries patrol officer		
1977—Federal task force recommends fish enhancement programs if tribes will stop catching steelhead	**1977**—Seattle is second busiest container port in U.S. and sixth busiest among world ports	
1979—U.S. Supreme Court upholds Boldt Decision	**1977**—Legislature passes law banning supertankers on inner Sound. Governor Dixy Lee Ray vetoes bill	
1980—U.S. District Court decides Indian tribes have right to voice in decisions on environmental development	**1979**—Hood Canal Bridge sinks in storm	

Bibliographic Notes

This is not meant to be a complete bibliography, just an indication of the sources I found most useful. They are not necessarily sources that will be useful—or available—to anyone else. The written records on which I relied for the earlier periods are all in major libraries, but for later periods I relied heavily on people's memories and private files, many of which may be inaccessible.

Chapter 1   **trees to cut and water to float them on**
The main source of information about the coming of Pope and Talbot to Hood Canal is the corporate history, *Time, Tide and Timber* by Edwin T. Coman, Jr., and Helen M. Gibbs (Palo Alto: Stanford University Press, 1949). For more general information about the early lumber industry on the Pacific Coast, I consulted *Mills and Markets* by Thomas R. Cox (Seattle: University of Washington Press, 1974). Specific quotes from and information about William Renton and the Port Blakely Mill Company come from the Port Blakely Mill Company papers in the University of Washington library, and Richard C. Berner's "The Port Blakely Mill Company, 1876–89," Pacific Northwest Quarterly (October 1966, pp. 158–171). A very valuable source of information about the early development of communities around the Sound is the *Puget Sound Business Directory and Guide to Washington Territory* (Olympia: Murphy and Harned, 1872), which I found in the Washington State Library. For information specifically about the development of Seattle as a port, I used Padraic Burke's *A History of the Port of Seattle* (Seattle: Port of Seattle, 1976) and *The Port of Seattle Yearbook* for 1914. Roger Sale's *Seattle: Past to Present* (Seattle: University of Washington Press, 1976) provides some general ideas about the development of Seattle. The diaries of Captain Henry Roeder, chiefly little more than account books, are in the University of Washington library.

Chapter 2   **a new economic geography**
The Port Blakely Mill Company papers and "The Port Blakely Mill Company, 1876–89," were useful for this period, too, as was *Mills and Markets*, which contains information about the evolution of logging tools. A complete history of the Pacific Northwest fishing industry is generally hard to come by, but a good source is *Fisheries of the North Pacific* by Robert J. Browning (Anchorage: Alaska-Northwest Publishing Company, 1974). The *Seattle Daily Intelligencer* quote is from the issue of September 10, 1878.

Chapter 3   **instead of prosperity . . . stagnation and despair**
The Port Blakely Mill Company papers are still useful, as are the St. Paul and Tacoma Lumber Company papers, also in the University of Washington library. My main source of information about the establishment of the Bremerton navy yard was the excerpt of official navy history in *Kitsap County History* (Silverdale, Washington: Kitsap County Historical Society, 1977). I found the John Muir quote not in the original, but in *Washington: Readings in the History of the Evergreen State* by Kent D. Richards, Raymond A. Smith, Jr., and Burton J. Williams (Lawrence, Kansas: Coronado Press, 1977). Robinson's reminiscence appears in a letter to Edwin G. Ames in the University of Washington library's Edwin G. Ames collection. My source for the history of populism and Washington's role as a prosilver state was Richard Hofstadter's *The Age of Reform* (New York: Alfred A. Knopf, 1955). The *Seattle Post-Intelligencer* for September and October 1892 provided a lot of interesting information in addition to the major stories I quote.

Chapter 4   **into the 20th century**
Griggs' correspondence is in the St. Paul and Tacoma Lumber Company papers. Other information about or related to the lumber industry came from *Mills and Markets* and the Weyerhaeuser corporate history, *Timber and Men* by Ralph W. Hidy, Frank Ernest Hill, and Allen Nevins (New York: Macmillan, 1963). I used Volume I of Mark Sullivan's *Our Times* (New York: Charles Scribner's Sons, 1926) for general background about the period and the *Age of Reform* for some information about the formation of trusts. Archie Binns's recollections of the wobblies appeared in *The Roaring Land* (New York: Robert M. McBride & Co., 1942). Information about the establishment of the Seattle Central Labor Council came from *The Seattle General Strike* by Robert L. Friedheim (Seattle: University of Washington Press, 1964). Some general background about the labor movement came from A. MacDonald's "Seattle's Economic Development, 1880–1910" (Ph.D. dissertation, University of Washington, 1959).

  J. C. Ford expressed his fears about the seamen's union in a letter to Congressman (later Senator) Wesley L. Jones, which is in the Wesley L. Jones collection in the University of Washington library. *Kitsap County History* and *A History of the Port of Seattle* were useful once again. The history of the fishing industry was drawn from a number of different sources: *Fisheries of the North Pacific; The Pacific Fisherman Yearbook* for 1914 (Seattle); a letter from John Cobb to H. M. Smith, which is in the University of Washington archives' John Cobb collection; an article by Cobb entitled "Pacific Halibut Fishery Declining," *Transactions of the American Fisheries Society* (June 1916, pp. 129–136); and a personal conversation with Joe Green.

Chapter 5   **the automobile commenced to dig in**
Background about the lumber industry came from Norman Clark's excellent *Mill Town* (Seattle: University of Washington Press, 1970). Trade statistics and some general information came from various editions of the *Port of Seattle Yearbook*. Sources of information about the general strike were *The Seattle General Strike* and "The Week Seattle Stopped," *The Weekly* (published in Seattle, February 7, 1979). Some general sense of what people were doing at the end of the war, as well as specific facts about Vashon came from the *Vashon Island News Record* of 1918 and 1919. Sources for the Jones Act included: the Wesley L. Jones collection; *American Shipping Policy* by Paul Maxwell Zeiss (Princeton: Princeton University Press, 1938); "A Political Biography of Wesley

L. Jones" by William Stuart Forth (Ph.D. dissertation, University of Washington, 1962); "The American Shipping Industry Since 1914" by John G. B. Hutchins, *The Business Historical Review* (June 1954, pp. 105–127); and *The New York Times* of August 9–13, 1920. Information about local transportation at the end of the war came from *Kitsap County History* and the Edwin G. Ames collection, which contains Ames' correspondence with Joshua Green.

Chapter 6   **water pollution had arrived**
General information about the development of the lumber industry came from *Timber and Men; Washington: A Bicentennial History* by Norman Clark (New York: W. W. Norton, 1976); and from Clark's *Mill Town*. The latter also supplied facts about the coming of the pulp industry to Shelton. Further information about developments in Shelton came from the Mark Reed correspondence in the University of Washington library; *The Story of Rayonier Incorporated* by Russell F. Erickson (New York: The Newcomen Society, 1963); and telephone conversations with Roger Tollefson, manager, environmental systems, ITT-Rayonier. The Pacific Coast Oyster Growers' Association papers in the University of Washington library tell a lot about the conflicts between oystermen and pulp mills, as do the Mark Reed papers and *The Rise and Decline of the Olympia Oyster Industry* by E. N. Steele (Elma, Washington: Fulco Publications, 1957). Further information came from conversations with Tollefson, Charles Woelke of the Washington State Department of Fisheries, Cedric Lindsay, the Department's former assistant director for shellfish, and Wayne Bruner, who supplied the memories of Anacortes. I also benefited from a letter written by Michael Waldichuk, director of the West Vancouver Laboratory of Fisheries and Ocean Canada in West Vancouver, B.C., and a brief conversation with the historian Robert E. Ficken.

Chapter 7   **give this great natural resource back to the people**
Conversations with Joe Green and Ken McLeod were extremely useful, and McLeod also supplied me with a copy of the pro–Initiative–77 brochure. Other sources included the *History of King County, Washington* by Clarence B. Bagley (Chicago and Seattle: S. J. Clarke Publishing Company, ca. 1929); *The Salmon: their fight for survival* by Anthony Netboy (Boston: Houghton Mifflin, 1974); *The Pacific Salmon Fisheries* by James A. Crutchfield and Giulio Pontecorvo (Baltimore: The Johns Hopkins Press, 1969); and the pre–1934 election issues of the *Seattle Post-Intelligencer* and *Vashon Island News Record*. The story about Boeing's new bomber appeared in the *Seattle Post-Intelligencer* of July 17, 1935.

Chapter 8   **the magnificent body of water was now in the way**
The figures about wartime growth came from a 1943 report by Washington's Secretary of State, contained in *Washington: Readings in the History of the Evergreen State*. The source of the postwar descriptions was, of course, *The New Washington: A Guide to the Evergreen State* by the Writers' Program (Portland, Oregon: U.S. Work Projects Administration, 1950). Economic information came from "Appraisal of the Pacific Northwest" by Maurice W. Lee, *Harvard Business Review* (May 1948, pp. 282–304). The long saga (1947–1951) of the state's acquisition of the ferry system was covered extensively by the *Seattle Post-Intelligencer* and *Vashon Island News Record*. I also looked at "Ferryboat Operator Gives In," *Business Week* (September 18, 1948, pp. 41–42). The current president of Black Ball Transport, Lois Acheson, helped me sort out which Black Ball Line was which. Logging figures came from *Economic Growth of the Puget Sound Region* (San Francisco: Arthur D. Little, Inc., 1964).

Chapter 9 **economic rationality had nothing to do with it**
The major sources were *Fisheries of the North Pacific* and *Salmon Gear Limitation in Northern Washington Waters* by William F. Royce, Donald E. Bevan, James A. Crutchfield, Gerald J. Paulik, and Robert L. Fletcher (Seattle: University of Washington Press, 1963). A conversation with Joe Green and the *1977–1978 Progress Report of the Pacific Fishery Management Council* (Portland, Oregon) were also useful.

Chapter 10 **free to dump anything**
The Pacific Coast Oyster Growers' Association papers contain many of the relevant studies and clippings. I also relied on personal conversations with Slade Gorton, Tom Wimmer, James Ellis, Ken McLeod, Roger Tollefson, Cedric Lindsay, Charles Woelke, E. O. Edmundson, George Anderson, and various individual fishermen.

Chapter 11 **images of the future**
Written sources of information included: Seattle: *Past to Present; The Economic Base of the Puget Sound Region Present and Future* by William Bunge (Washington State Department of Commerce and Economic Development, 1960); *Ocean Related Industries' Impact on Puget Sound* (Economic Development Council of Puget Sound, Seattle Chamber of Commerce, City of Seattle, Port of Seattle, 1978); *Washington Public Ports Association Washington Port System Study* (Seattle: Reid, Middleton & Associates, 1975); and "The Maritime Industry's Magic Box" by Patrick Douglas, *Seattle* (May 1969, pp. 52–55). I also relied heavily on conversations with officials of the Port of Seattle, the Port of Olympia, and the Port Authority of New York and New Jersey. Some figures came from *Economic Growth of the Puget Sound Region*.

Chapter 12 **the tribes got half the fish**
The sources for this chapter included Boldt's decision in *U.S. vs. Washington*, the extensive coverage given the fishing rights controversy in the Seattle press, and eleven years' worth of conversations with white fishermen, Indian fishermen, attorneys, congressional staff members, and officials of Indian tribes and the state and federal governments. Richard Rathbun's views on Indian fishing rights appear in *A Review of the Fisheries in the Contiguous Waters of the State of Washington and British Columbia* (Washington: Government Printing Office, 1899).

Chapter 13 **the opening wedge**
The coming of the aluminum industry to Whatcom County is described very well in "Intalco: The Whatcom Massacre" by Mary Kay Becker, *The Seattle Flag* (April 26, 1972). My main source for the Guemes Island conflict was "Paradise Lost?" by Dolly Connely, Seattle (October 1966, pp. 48–51). Information about the hydrofoil episode came from personal observations and conversations plus running coverage in the *Vashon-Maury Island Beachcomber* (1977). Conversations with Tom Wimmer, William Van Ness, and Don Hopps provided useful information about passage of the shoreline management initiative and the state and federal Environmental Policy Acts. Additional information about the shoreline initiative (August 1970) and the Everett pulp mill closings (January 1972) came from *The Seattle Times*.

Chapter 14   **clear for a hundred fathoms down**
Sources for this chapter included: the transcript of hearings on an oil port in
Puget Sound held in 1976 by the Washington State House of Representatives'
Transportation and Utilities Committee; the *Congressional Record* for October
4 and 5, 1977; regular coverage throughout the 1970s of the oil issue by the
Seattle press and *Northwest Passage;* conversations with, among others, Robert
Lynette; former anti-supertanker lobbyists Dan Seligman and Martin Baker;
former members of Warren Magnuson's staff; and Washington State Representative Mary Kay Becker. Belinda Pearson and Jackie Etsall of Seattle First National Bank provided useful economic background about water-oriented activities.

Index

Photographs for *The Water Link* were provided by the following institutional photo collections:

University of Washington Libraries
  Historical Photo Collection (HPCUW)
  Northwest Collection (UWNWC)
  Manuscripts Collection (UWMC)

Museum of History & Industry
  Historical Society of Seattle & King County (HSSKC)
  Puget Sound Maritime Historical Society/Williamson Collection (PSMHS/WC)

Whatcom Museum of History & Art, Photo Collection (WMHA)

University of Washington News Service (UW)

Tacoma Public Library (TPL)

Northwest Room Everett Public Library/Juleen Collection (NREPL)

National Marine Fisheries Service (NMFS)

Other photographs were provided by the Boeing Company, Port of Seattle, *Seattle Times*, *Seattle Post Intelligencer*, Ken McLeod, Frank Denman, Dale Blindheim, Intalco, MARCO, METRO, and *Seattle Magazine*.